C000303338

RANGERS I.C.F.

RANGERS I.C.F.

DAVEY CARRICK AND MARTIN KING

HEAD-HUNTER BOOKS

First published in September 2006 by Head-Hunter Books

Copyright © 2006 Martin King and Davie Carrick

Photographs copyright © 2006
Davie Carrick and Martin King
Front cover: Kortney King
Cartoons: Ben Marsh

The publisher has made every effort to contact
the newspapers for the use of the cuttings

The moral right of the author has been asserted

All rights reserved. No part of this publication may be reproduced in any form or
by any means without permission in writing from the publisher, nor be otherwise
circulated in any form of binding or cover other than that in which it is published
and without a similar condition being imposed on the subsequent purchaser.

ISBN 0 9548542 8 4

Head-Hunter Books

FOREWORD

BY IRVINE WELSH

When my old buddy Martin King asked me to do a foreword for this book, my first reaction was something along the lines of ' there's no way I'm doing anything for some two- bob weedgie mob'. However when I learned it was Davie Carrick who was the author, I quickly changed my mind. I first met Davie at a good few year's back at a wedding of a mutual friend, and he's an excellent guy, who'll tell the story of the Rangers casual firm without bullshit or self- aggrandisement. Davie is very much liked, and respected by many lads from other firms, precisely for these qualities. Loyalists and sectarian politics have never floated his boat, and he was always happy to be a lad that ran with his mob, with no hidden agenda outside the Saturday sport partaken in by so many, since the game began in Scotland.

All grounds evidenced disquiet about the casual's emergence in the eighties. Even old school football thugs of my generation were unable to understand the idea of not wearing colours. They were amongst the most vocal opponents to the then younger mob. "It's magic you know Hibees and casuals don't go," was one chant at Easter Road favoured by cavemen, and they disdained them in the same way that veteran cashies now sneer at the young team, uniform in their Burburry and Stone Island and their claim to be casuals. The casual movement must have met more resistance in Glasgow as it was seen as a east coast phenomenon, which challenged Rangers and Celtic as Scotland's traditional hooligan bastions. For a city that has prided itself on its style, this was never traditionally evidenced of Glasgow's ` Christmas tree` supporters. The preoccupation with the politics of Northern Ireland amongst Rangers and Celtic fans meant that the uniform was all banners, flags, scarves, badges and which had the club colours. Loyalism the major cultural influence at Ibrox, even its advocates would concede, is about tradition, which is the opposite to fashion. That Rangers and to a lesser extent Celtic even managed to produce casual firms, then, is something of an anomaly in itself. Like many of his contemporaries, Davie leads a quiet life these days, but is well placed to reflect back on the formation of the Rangers mob largely as a response to the dominant crews of Aberdeen and Hibernian and the emergence of the casual movement in Glasgow. So while this book will be primarily be of interest to Rangers fans and people in Glasgow, it may also achieve wider reference from everybody, who has been touched in some way by the phenomenon, we still call football hooliganism. That is, just about anyone who has attended a game of football in the U.K.

This book is dedicated to my son Jamie
who missed out every Saturday
through football.

ACKNOWLEDGEMENTS

Firstly big thanks to Sandy who probably did more for the book then me.

I would like to mention the following people: Harky, Rab Anderson, Baz, Broony, Warren, Eddie Carr, James Collins, Deek, Sweeton, Jeff, Terry and his boy Bob, Strachan, Mark H, Geo, Scott Newlands, Moose, Pedro, Peter K, Stevie Mc F, (Woodhill) Dyne, Big Mark, Geemas, My brother Brien, A Christie, Ricky, Scott Mclean, Jim Hamilton, Evil Jim, Jock, Big Paul G, Big al, Andy Kenny, Curry, Nail, Finn, Eck, Big Gary (fae Straanrar) Graig , Gary, Brien, / the faarin Brothers, Paul Lamon Adds, Skelly, Paul Wilson, Elloit, Craw, Colin Bell, Murray, Danny, Steelie, Jack, Joe, English Steve, Dave Elders, Wilson, Matthew, Willie Craig, Wee Andy, Riot, Davie Carmicheal, Cass, Kenny, Con, Smiler, Scott Ingles, Rab Mcguir, Fergie, Laverty, Jamie, Stevie Campbell, Mckay.

MAN CITY - John, Stewart,Raymon, Paul & Peter, Monkey, Mickey Francis (Thanks for letting us use your club)

CELTIC – Jerry, Russel, Sean K, Steph F, Melso, Fedgie, Flash, Gaga.

HIBS – Mcleod, McNulty, Mickey, Hendo.

HEARTS – Bobby Thomson, Gags, Dallas, Greg.

SHEFFIELD UNITED – Flynnie, John.

CHELSEA – Fat Pat, Tony Murphy, Cutler, Nightmare, Jason Marriner, Chris C (Who I first met at Kings Cross v Leeds), The Twins, Big Geoff for his contribution and Ben Marsh for the cartoons

CARDIFF – Neil.

The Coventry boys who've got a good boy now in Geemac.

THESE BOYS SADLY NO LONGER WITH US
BARRY JOHNSTON – WELLSEY – PANDY – DAVIE COLLINS
JOHN MCNAIR – JASON (GINGER) CARDIFF – DINO (HIBS)
KEDDIE (HIBS) – TONY F (CELTIC) – COLIN (PETERBOROUGH)

CONTENTS

CHAPTER 1

WELCOME TO SPRINGBURN

I was born 40 years ago in Springburn, which is just north of Glasgow. It's almost like the rest of Glasgow where there is a mixture of Protestants and Catholics. It's a tough area. I was born in my mum and dad's tenement flat, the sort of building where the half a dozen families that lived there would all share the one toilet and bathroom. My brother, Brian, is a year older than me so four of us lived in this more than modest abode. My dad was a train driver and mum was a housewife. It was tough but we never went without like some families did. We'd go on holiday all over the country using my dad's rail pass. I remember going all the way down to the Isle of Wight and another time over to the Isle of Man. We had some good times.

Lots of people from Springburn were employed by the railway. There was a rail depot close by so a good few people were kept in employment.

At an early age I noticed the gang fights that went on around the streets in my area and in some cases there would be up to a 100 people per side, and there were some right old battles.

My first school was Balornock Primary School and by this time my family had moved to a 25 storey high-rise flat and very posh and modern it was too. We'd definitely gone up in the world! We had our very own bathroom and toilet and panoramic views of Glasgow. From the various windows inside the flat you could see Ibrox, Hampden and Parkhead. It was an amazing view. The flats were brand new and there was no graffiti on the walls in the lobby or the smell of piss in the lifts. I loved the place and I remember my mum and dad being all excited about moving there.

I found school really hard work. I wasn't interested in any of the subjects and that included P.E. and football. I was a bit of a dreamer. I played football out in the street with the rest of the kids but to be honest I was just shit.

Dad liked his Saturday night and Sunday lunch time drinking sessions. He loved a pint or two but he never came home nasty. He was just so funny and full of nonsense. He was a joker. I remember seeing him cut across a new by-pass they were building behind our flats and as he came back from the pub he was tripping up on the bricks which were lying around and treading in half opened bags of cement, and piles of sand. He was like a half pissed Frank Spencer! When he got back up to the flat he was covered in mud and dust and had grass stains on the back of his trousers where he'd slipped down a muddy embankment. I have great memories of my dad who sadly died a few years back.

The first bit of bother I got into with the police was when I was about 13. A police car drove past and I smashed the window with a brick. There was a gang of about 10 of us and we all ran off but the police caught hold of a couple of us. The police arrested us and gave us a right talking; to before taking me home where later I got good belting off me dad.

For the last year at secondary school I just never bothered going. My mate's mum had a job as a cleaner so she was out the house early doors, so I used to get up early and make out I was off to school and then go around his place and sniff glue. Everybody I know was doing it. When I did turn up for school I sat up the back and paid no attention of what was going on in the class. Id sit there sniffing glue, not giving a fuck who could see me. It was like taking L.S.D. It had a similar effect on you and I used to get out of my nut on it.

Around this time I was a bit of a punk and I was into all the music. I loved it. I'd listen to the Sex Pistols, The Clash and The Damned. I was also into The Exploited, who was a top Scottish punk band. I was right into the whole scene. One time I had me hair cut into a Mohican. Me and me mates used to meet down at the Virgin mega-store on Union Street down in the town. One Saturday about 150 Aberdeen Casuals came into town on their way to Motherwell for a game. This was in the days before Rangers had an organized mob. We were all quite young but this Aberdeen lot were anything from late teens to late twenties, with a sprinkling of even older guys that looked like oil rig workers. Anyway our rag tag mob have started a row and run this Aberdeen firm everywhere. I think we must have been off the glue this particular day because we had our wits about us.

Because of my sniffing glue activities I'd been sent to see the school psychiatrist. Loads of us were walking around like zombies, at times it was like a scene from the spoof horror film `Sean of the Dead, or a scene from the old black and white film `Dawn of the Dead`. He asked me a load of questions about myself, things like "how did I feel?" and "what's it like growing up?" It was a complete load of nonsense. I think they had to show they were trying to do something about the massive glue problem but I don't know who was kidding who with their daft questions and my even dafter answers. To me it was just a phase I was going through. I looked at it as a part of growing up.

The last year there I just never turned up at school so the rule was if I found employment I could legally leave school early, before I was 16, so I managed to get an apprenticeship as a welder burner in the Govan Ship Builders. I used to have to get a bus into the city centre and another bus to right outside the main gates. I got the job through the careers office at school and I think they were well pleased to get rid of me. I had to do a little bit of an intelligence test to get the job and I even amazed myself by passing with flying colours. It was the same shipyard where the comedian Billy Connelly used to work and in his act he tells about how the shipyard had to take on as apprentices a percentage of disabled folk. At the end of the working day and because there was thousands of people working there, they'd let the less able-bodied people out first. Anybody passing on the bus must have seen all these people coming out of the gates limping and in wheel chairs and thought to themselves "fucking hell, how hard does that shipyard work these poor people?"

Anyway, Billy Connelly tells it brilliantly. There must have been a couple of hundred coming out at once and I know you shouldn't laugh, but it did look funny. It looked like the land of the living dead. The piss taking when any new lads started was unbelievable. Young boys were sent off to the stores to get a box of sparks or a glass hammer or striped paint and you didn't know at the time it was a big piss take and you'd go off and do it! But we were taught a proper trade and started off in a classroom or training room where you were taught the basics of cutting and welding. We'd cut holes into metal and make silly things like metal dumbbells but it was all good stuff and it taught us to get a feel for the tools.

The basic wage was only £22 a week but you had a subsidized canteen and the food wasn't too bad.

Ship building on the Clyde in those days was massive but over the years with closures and redundancies ship building in Glasgow has been in decline. I only stayed there a couple of months because basically I was sick of hearing how much money my mates were making in their jobs compared to what I was getting a week. Dad wasn't too happy when I told him and said I shouldn't listen to other people and that what they were claiming to be earning was probably total bollocks. Why was I jacking in a perfectly good job, which would give me a trade at the end of it? Why was I leaving a good job only to go into some dead-end job with no prospects? Funny thing was I knew he was right. I ended up getting a job at an electrics warehouse selling aerials and cassettes and other bits and pieces, and then I got put working on the trade counter. It was more money than the ship builders, plus I was alot happier, but mum and dad weren't impressed. "Stupid dead-end job" the old man used to say.

I stayed there for near on two years and I made a good few bob there. I had a right little scam going on with the regular customers and let's just say they were happy and so was I.

Around this time I got my first criminal conviction. I was charged with police assault and criminal damage. I'd been drinking in the local pubs around town since I was 15 so I thought that I could hold my drink. I was a seasoned boozer, or so I thought. I came out of a dance this particular night and started arguing with the bouncers outside. I was a right pest and a gobby fucker and I loved a fight. I classed myself as a good fighter. Not being big headed or nothing but

I could handle myself. I wouldn't back down from no one and in some peoples eyes I may have been getting a bit of a reputation. When I was 16 to 17 I was the same build or weight as I am now. I'd never boxed or done karate or judo or kung fu but as I say I was as game as they come. I was a street fighter. I think my dad had been a bit fiery in his younger days but he didn't like to talk about it. I was my own man.

Me and me mate had come out of the club when I realized I'd left my jacket in there. I went to go back in there but the bouncers weren't having it and shut and locked the glass doors and stood behind them laughing at me. I went fucking mad and lobbed a bottle at them, which bounced off the glass and smashed on the pavement. Next minute the doors have flown open and out they've come. That was it. I was off and they've chased us up the road. I'm steaming drunk and all I'm concentrating on is staying on the path and on my feet and not tripping up on the kerb. Next minute someone's grabbed me and we're swapping punches. The thing was, and what I didn't know, at the time but it was two plain-clothes policemen that had grabbed hold of me. So that was that. I ended up going to court and told my side of the story but the judge wasn't interested and I got 210 hours community service. How did I know they were plain clothes police? I was pissed for fucks sake!

I think I may have been a bit of a rebel because I never really got any affection at home from my mum or dad. I can never recall getting any cuddles or being shown any real love. I know that's no excuse but I think that could have helped me as I grew up.

I was into the early 80s music in a big way, bands like Human League, Duran Duran, Spandau Ballet, Depeche Mode have all stood the test of time and still sound good to this day. I liked the music but the clothes that went with it weren't for me. All them frilly shirt and baggy trousers, waistcoats and head bands, red pixie boots and a silk scarf tied around your head or tied back to front around your neck. I wasn't into the NEW Romantic look! I never wanted to be Simon Le Bon, and I still don't. Japan was another band I was into and went to one of their concerts in '82. I loved my live music and also saw the likes of Pink Floyd at Man City's Maine Road, and New Order. Liverpool seemed to churn out quite a few bands in the early 80s with most of them half decent. You had Echo and the Bunnymen, Teardrop Explodes and China Crisis to name just three.

One thing I have to thank me dad for and that was getting me started supporting Rangers. He first took me and me brother when I was about 9 and I remember one of my first games at Ibrox was against Italian side, Juventus, in a European game. I used to save all the programmes and kept a scrapbook for years and it was only recently that an angry ex girlfriend threw it away. I had all the Rangers posters and players pictures on my bedroom walls. I'd lay in bed of a night and my favourite players like John Greg, Alex McDonald, Bobby Russell, Tom Forsyth, Sandy Jardine and Davie Cooper would be up there looking down at me.

We went through a wee spell when the crowds were down and Ibrox wasn't sold out, for certain games. One season, dad got me and my brother season tickets for the main stand, we were only about 14. We were at Jim Stewart's testimonial against Dundee United and we lost 4-1 and it was a very poor attendance. Those were crazy days.

CHAPTER 2

THE I.C.F.

Around about 1980 I started going to Ibrox with about 20 mates from around my area. We'd meet up in a local pub and then catch the bus into the city centre and then have a scout about for any fans from other teams. The Skinhead look was big then with some people with shaved heads and the fashion was wearing green or blue zip up, collarless, nylon, flight jackets with the orange coloured lining. Topped off with ox-blood high legged Doctor Martens, half way up their legs and with their jeans, meeting the boots just below the knee so plenty of the boot was visible.

Music wise these boys were into 2-Tone, which was a Ska revival. The Specials, a Midland based band, led the scene (later to become the Fun Boy Three) along with The Beat who later went on to form Fine Young Cannibals, and of course the Nutty Boys themselves, Madness. I remember the original skins when I was just a little kid. They wore Crombie overcoats or Harrington jackets, Ben Sherman shirts and Levi Sta-prest worn at half-mast, with shiny leather brogues or Doctor Marten boots. They would hang about on the street corners encouraging us wee youngsters to attack the local catholic school, which was just up the road from my school. A couple of times it did go off between the two schools with either us going to attack them or them coming down to sort us out. It would be one big mass bundle with no one getting really hurt. It was more handbags at ten paces and maybe the odd bloody nose, but no serious injuries. It was all good fun and if one of them turned up wearing a Celtic scarf then that would be grabbed and paraded as a victory trophy, a scalp worthy of any John Wayne fighting Red Indian.

In my teenage years following Rangers we'd drink in `The District Bar` over near Ibrox before going into the game. We'd stand on the Copeland Road terrace, which was the equivalent of The Jungle at Celtic or The Shed at Chelsea. That was where all the singers and poseurs would gather. It was the place to be seen. It was where, if you were somebody or wanted to be somebody, you'd stand. Then the new stand was built so the boys moved over to the west enclosure. Before the game we'd get into one of the pubs or bars along Paisley Road West and have a few beers. Nearly all of us were underage but the District Bar was one of our favourites and it's still there.

There's not many pubs actually near to the ground but there is one which is a bit of a Celtic pub so the least said about that the better. Everybody sang who stood in the West enclosure and week by week, game by game, our gang would seem to grow. At first you'd be on nodding terms with a few familiar faces and then you'd exchange a "hello" or "how ya doing?" and then you'd see them over the course of a few games and then you'd have a bit of a chat with them.

I tried chasing the girls but never seemed to get anywhere so I stuck with me mates watching Rangers. I was also into my clothes and fashion around this time and in Glasgow we had `The Warehouse` which was a great men's clothes shop which stocked all the latest designer labels. But there wasn't a great deal of choice for up to date fashion in Glasgow. Now adays you have a lot more men's shops with places like `Cruise` selling all the latest gear.

Football wasn't the only place you were guaranteed a punch up. Night clubs in Glasgow could always be a bit lively. I'd been going into the clubs since I was about 15. One night I was in `Studs` night-club and on one side of the dance floor was all the boys from Springburn and up the other end was a gang from Maryhill, which was about 10 minutes from Springburn. All of a sudden the whole place has gone up with glasses and bottles and tables and chairs flying through the air. A few knives were flashed but that was nothing new in Glasgow.

Glasgow has always had this association with knife crime. Knives, for some reason, have always been associated with Glasgow be it with criminals or the underworld or Teddyboys or Skinheads. The youth and sometimes the O.A.P.s of Glasgow have never been afraid to use a blade. I carried one myself for years and wouldn't have been afraid to use it. Just walking home of a night knowing you had a knife on you made you feel a bit safer. Sometimes you have to fight fire with fire.

I got caught around this time for pinching scrap metal. A lot of the old tenement buildings were being pulled down and me and a mate climbed onto one of the sites and loaded up with all the old scrap lead, copper and brass, but we ended up getting caught by the police. I went to court and got a ticking off and a fine. It was just pure daft things wee boys got up to, it was as simple as that. I was at that age where I never seemed to be at home. I was either around my latest girlfriend's or sleeping on mates' floors or settees.

As I say I was earning well at the electrical warehouse and some days I was making £40 on the side, a lot of money in those days. It was brilliant times. My work mates were a few years older and we'd jump the train and go through to Edinburgh and have a weekend over there. Aberdeen was another good week-end away as it's only three hours from Glasgow by train. Another mate's sister worked in a clothes shop so we'd have a bit of a deal with her and wear things like leather suits to the trendy clubs around town. We thought we were the dogs' bollocks and looking back we must have looked like The Pet Shop Boys. Still, who hasn't looked back in horror at being a fashion victim? Anyone who says otherwise is a liar?

I've also been to Blackpool a few times with me mates, and that can be a real laugh. For the first two weeks in August you'd think Glasgow was shut, as it could be that quiet as half the population seemed to head south to Blackpool. There's lots of booze downed in that fortnight and plenty of fights. I went a couple of times with Steph Farley who was a good mate of mine and used to go with Celtic's mob. Gary Hamilton, another mate of mine, ended up signing for Middlesbrough when he was 15. Rangers and Celtic both wanted him but they both couldn't match what he'd been offered at Boro. I used to go down and see him and after he'd earned a few bob he'd drive back up here in his red, two-door Mercedes convertible. He's now coaching somewhere out in Texas. I went to his wedding and Stuart Ripley, his Boro team mate, was there and we got chatting and he told me he'd spoken to Celtic about a possible million pound transfer. He'd been up for talks and he fancied the move. That was until I put him off and the deal then fell through. We'd had a good chat over a few beers and he finally saw sense. He was a good lad and good company but in my view was a shit player who was very light-weight. He ended up moving to Blackburn Rovers and if I remember rightly he was there when they won the title under Kenny Dalglish and Ray Harford. So in the end he did have a Celtic connection.

I got in a bit more trouble with the police one night over in Bishop-Briggs. There was a bit of trouble outside the pub and a policeman got pushed through a hedge and landed on a metal pole and fucked himself. What we didn't know was that there had been a stabbing earlier on that night and there was undercover police sitting watching us from a nearby car park in unmarked cars. I was grabbed and thrown into the back of a police car. We'd been originally stopped for nothing by the police, who were very arrogant and were horrible and just looking for trouble. One of them said something to me and I told him to get a life and to get the fuck because we'd done nothing wrong so with that he's grabbed me and he's come off worse as he's gone through the hedge. When I was in the back of the police car one of them's jumped into the back of the car and started punching me around the head. Another's got in the front seat and drove off while this other cunts punching the fuck out of me. I did no more and leant back in the seat lifted one of my legs up and kicked the driver in the back of the head, which caused him to jolt forward and lose control of the steering wheel, crash into some parked cars, bounce off them and then hit a wall. A support unit turned up and dragged me out and threw me into the back of their van and then I thought I was going to die as they beat me black and blue. They proper leathered me. They punched and beat me around the body and in my face. There was blood everywhere and I can honestly say it was the worse doing I've every had in my life. I was fucked good and proper. I had handcuffs on so there wasn't a lot I could do. These bastards were vicious. When we got to the police station it didn't end there. I was dragged in by my hair and was punched and kicked. I was thrown headfirst into the front reception desk which broke my nose and busted my lip. The sergeant at the desk didn't even look up from what he was doing as the beating continued. I was thrown into a cell and my handcuffs were taken off and then I just went mental and lost the plot. I was kicking and punching the cell door and calling the coppers all the cunts under the sun. In the end they could put up with it no more and called a unit up from Baird Street, which is the main police station in Glasgow, to come and take me down there. They have the reputation of being hard bastards who take no nonsense from anyone. The cell door opened and I stepped back. I had my hands free now so it would be a much fairer contest. I took in a deep breath and shaped up to them but wave after wave of them bundled on top of me and pinned me down. One big cunt amongst them placed his knee on my balls. "Can you feel where my knee is?" he growled. "Oh aye" I replied and stopped struggling. There was no point. I was fucked. I was put back in handcuffs and taken away. I was given a wet cloth to clean myself up with but no doctor was called and no-one checked on my injuries. I saw a solicitor and I was given a P.F. release, which meant I wasn't allowed to go up in front of a judge with these injuries. I was released but still charged.

My whole ear was black and swollen. In the end I had to drop my case against the police because the independent witness I originally had in my defence couldn't be traced. He'd moved or something so in the end I had no evidence to proceed against the police. I was charged with assault on the police and received community service and a fine. I did hear that the copper who originally started all of it was out to make a name for himself and got into so much bother he was transferred to another nick.

At Rangers we had a couple of West Ham lads that came up to Ibrox to sell the B.N.P. and the N.F. papers. This was about '83 and it was the start of the Casual movement at Rangers. Barry Johnstone, Wee Wellsey and Andy, who jumped off a bridge into the Clyde, were the main faces in getting our firm up and running but sadly all three of them are no longer with us. The West Ham lads told us their tales of taking The Shed at Chelsea and clearing the C.B.L. at Millwall's Den. Their mob was called The I.C.F. (The Inter City Firm) named after the mode of transport they took to away games. They chose to avoid taking the British Rail football specials and instead went under their own steam on the regular, more modern, Inter-city trains.

At the time we had no organized mob so to speak of and we were so unorganized, for a big club it was laughable. Right back at the start of things we'd go to somewhere like Aberdeen and there'd be maybe three football specials going up there. We'd all turn up at Glasgow station and there'd be kids, mums and dads with their Rangers scarves, Skinheads, Punks, and Mods. It was a right mish mash of support. No one would really know one another. We were like the Man Utd, of Scotland where thousands of us would turn up somewhere and take over the place. Windows would be smashed and rival fans chased off just because of our sheer weight of numbers. We'd take over towns and cities no problem and that's why, over the last 10 years, Aberdeen have been so nasty and so game, against us. That's because for years their youngsters saw their brothers, cousins and dads bullied by our huge, rampaging mob of beer monsters. They'd seen their boys punched to fuck and must have said to themselves enough is enough and they went and got themselves organized and nowadays give a good account of themselves and give as good as they get. They're fighting back, so to speak. We'd go anywhere and swamp them with numbers, Hearts, Hibs, Motherwell, Dundee. You name it, we'd take the piss. It wasn't really bullying but the Rangers support has always had this reputation. We never really had one mob from a certain part of Glasgow or one face that ran the show but Barry Johnstone took it upon himself to get things organized. Barry was younger than me and could handle himself. He was always a smart dresser and looked the part. He was a good looking fella who had no problem pulling the women. We all respected him, and he'd grab hold of you and he'd shout and get excited. I don't think he knew how to speak quietly. His voice could be heard above everyone elses. He was good fun to be with and a good all round lad.

We had some good boys who all seemed to come together at around the same time as the Rangers own version of The I.C.F. was born. It was not one person that decided to take that name, it just happened. Very quickly known faces in our firm came under the banner of The I.C.F. and soon our Casual mob numbered a good few hundred. We even put a mob together of well over a thousand at a game against Aberdeen. Boys came, not just from Glasgow but from Edinburgh, Stranrar, Falkirk, even south of the border, it really took off, it just snowballed. We were all dressed in Lois jeans, Kicker boots; it was an army with a fashion sense. We travelled everywhere and kept out of the way of the watchful eye of the police. Thousands of us in 86 headed down to Tottenham for their former player Paul Millers testimonial. We were everywhere. We climbed over two fences to get at the Spurs' fans, but they just weren't up for it. We went down the night before in a van and met up in Trafalgar Square. Outside the ground we ran them everywhere and every time we got near them outside after the game, they would not stand and fight. We ended up on the Broadwater Farm Estate and the locals put up a bit of a fight but we had such big numbers we just took the piss. I'd say numbers wise we were the biggest firm in Britain, at this time. I'd say we had more numbers than Man United. No one could touch us that was sure. Age wise we went from 13 years old up to mid thirties. It was a real mixed bag.

From the start I'd say I was a major face. I was well respected and had a lot of say in where we went, what time we met and so on. Barry was the same he was a good boy, and he was there at the start and he was there most of the time. We had a few handy boys in the mob that could handle themselves and we had a few who weren't afraid to use a blade. Wee Wellsey ended up in the high court for cutting a Celtic fan's throat and was found not guilty. We had a few notorious blade merchants. One time we were bad for it. One of the lads had a few calling cards printed with "You've just met the I.C.F" printed on them but it was all done as a joke. It was really copying the teams from down south. It never drew the attention of the police but there again we never really got any special attention from the Old Bill. We had the usual uniform police around on match days but there never was, as far as I know, any plain clothes following us about or any football intelligence unit on our case. The way it seemed to work was, if they caught you fighting they nicked you. It was as simple as that. No big stitch up court cases costing the taxpayers millions, no falsifying evidence or undercover operations, no dramas. They didn't really know us and we didn't know them and we kept it like that for a long, long time.

WARREN

I was born in Edinburgh and I'm 35 years of age I've been a Rangers fan all my life well basically from when I could first talk. My brother followed them and I done the same. The first game I ever went to was against St Mirren in 1982. I was about 12 and went with my brother. Davie Copper and the keeper Peter Mcloy were two favourites of mine. I went on a supporters bus, one particular bus, 'The Edinburgh Union Jack' is quite famous and still going strong and I know quite a few of the guys that still travel on it. That bus in the past as been attacked by Hibs fans, it had quite a history in the early days of the football casual. From then I first started seeing and meeting what we called 'The Dressers,' they caught my eye with their wedge haircuts and the Pringle jerseys and bright coloured track suits. I wanted to be just like them they stuck out a mile they were something different and they were vilified. We all stood in the West Enclosure, that's where all the singers and dressers went at Ibrox. It was still terracing in those days and most of the noise came from that part of the ground. Basically I just hung about and got to know a few of the lads, I saw the faces week in week out but because I was from

Edinburgh I was viewed in the early days with a bit of suspicion. As we used to spill out of the ground at the end of the match I just used to tag on at the end of the mob. I was there I got myself known and from there it just snowballed and I worked my way in and up the ladder and into the pecking order. It was as simple as that. It was a natural progression. I went to School with one of Hibs main lads who was a good mate of mine, he knew I was going to Rangers and so my name was being mentioned to the rest of the Hibs firm this propelled me into the limelight of the football world. I got myself known and they knew I was in existence. That was it from the early age of 14-15 I was known as one of Rangers boys. When Rangers played at Hibs or Hearts I got all the usual shit of tell your boys this or tell your boys that, at the end of the day I was a hate figure. With the Hearts lot I've always got on with most of them, although a few of their younger lot have got a bit mouthy at times. I knew a lot of the Hearts lads from the gang fights in the city and plus when it comes to the religious aspect we've on the same side of the fence. But with the Hibs lot I was always at loggerheads with them and I felt that I had to prove myself more against Hibs simply because I went with Rangers. In years gone by my mother and fathers house as been attacked and 4ft high graffiti and words sprayed on the outside walls. But that was done by the Republican element within the Hibs firm it was done not because of my support for Rangers but because of political differences and sectarianism. It all stemmed from the annual Republican parades that went through the City and the Hearts and the Rangers lads would always turn out to attack and oppose these marches. Their way of revenge was not to face me face to face but was to paint threats to kill, etc etc on my parent's house. I found out through the grapevine who, was responsible but as I say they couldn't do anything to my face and the thing was I never ever lived in that house. The only time they've ever called it on with me is when they've had superior numbers and hand on heart I've never been turned over by one of them, I've had a few close shaves but their main lads I could sit down and have a drink with them, no problem. They've proper lads, but its, this particular element that can't let this Republican thing go. I'd say The Rangers I.C.F. on their day were the top casual firm in Scotland. To me there was only two real firms and that was us and Hibs, Aberdeen have always like to think they have and in the past have tried to push themselves and talk their way to the top but numerical advantage does not equate to superiority, as far as I'm concerned they've always had the numbers and they could at times muster 600-700 in a mob, where as we've operated on having a right tight 60 or 70, top firm that get the results. Them ever having a top firm is bollocks as far as I'm concerned. I know a few of the Celtic lads and I was on holiday on the 12th of July in Lanzarote last year and bumped into Sean one of their main faces in a Rangers bar of all places. He couldn't' believe it he thought he was safe and that no body he knew would spot him. I was out celebrating the 12th of July but that didn't' stop us having a good drink and a good talk about football, and that's how it should be. He's a Republican and as extreme in his views as I am with mine but what over rides that is the fact that he is one of the boys and we share that respect and share that common sense. Plus we respect one another in football terms. He's a lad and a proper lad and I can see where he's coming from. They have a few good lads and at one time through their numbers used to run Glasgow city centre. But once we got organized in the 80s and 90s we took over. When it comes to a toe to toe they can't match Rangers. I have my own political views but I don't' believe in sectarianism. I have my views on race I have my views on religion but quite simply anyone born on these islands can change their religion at will but racially you cannot change where you come from. I don't' simply hate someone for what they are or where they come from that's just not me that view holds you back and gets you nowhere. I'd say the Rangers firm is the most patriotic and right leaning in their views then most other football firms in Britain. I never go to football now, simply because I've had two life bans, its pathetic, these people really are, its because of a changing of the guard. So to speak, I also received a letter from the club telling me I was banned for life after the trouble out in Holland at the PSV game. I am a proper fan not like some of the people that write these letters and introduce these bans some of them know fuck all about football and football fans. Up here if you've ever been or are a football hooligan then you're frowned upon down in England I'd say its more excepted up here your still vilified, you're looked upon as the anti-Christ. For a certain period of time I was never out of the papers if I was abroad or had done something then they were on my case its cost me 5 jobs over the years. I've had pictures of me appear in a certain paper where a mug shot of me as been taken by the police at the police station after I'd been arrested and charged with conspiracy of aiding and abetting. This charge came about after I was seen drinking with a few of the Chelsea lads who were up here for a pre-season friendly game with Hibs. How did those photos of me get into the hands of the press? There was 8 of arrested after we were dawn raided and had our front doors caved in. It doesn't take a rocket scientist to work out who's working with who? The authorities waste so much money on the football hooligan scene. One example was when I traveled down to London from Edinburgh on the 6-15am train. I was meeting the rest of the lads to go to a troops out march, there was a huge firm out amongst the football lads that day, and later on that evening the police approached my mate Browney and asked him where I'd gone. They told him in great detail where and at what time I'd started off that morning and also where I'd been all day. Frightening isn't it? And it makes you wonder? Big Brother is watching us. Basically they've middle aged men who are physically unfit for the job who get money for doing near on nothing, its like when these police spotters go abroad for the football its one big Jolly for them. It's all at the expense of the tax- payer. Give these people a proper job to do. How about them catching some burglars or some other pond life? Perhaps that's too easy, a? I still live in Edinburgh but I travel a lot with work but I still keep in touch with Davie who happens to be one of my best mates.

SMOOTHIE

I'm 45 years old and from Glasgow. I was bought up in a predominately Catholic area. It was 22% Protestant and the rest were Catholics. I went to a non-denominational school, as there's no such thing in Scotland as religious mixed schools. Catholic schools are state schools and they get money from the government to fund their schools.

I started going to football and watching Rangers when I was 16. All my family were big Rangers' fans but they were very Christian people. My mum was in the Salvation Army and was very easy going. She encouraged me to have both Catholic and Protestant friends.

At school we had different holidays to the Catholic kids. We'd get a day off for the Queen's birthday or a bank holiday and they'd get days off when it was some Saints' birthday.

I was off to school one day and I saw a Catholic kid I know off to his school carrying an envelope with some coins jangling about inside. He explained that there was a collection at school for black babies in Africa and that you could adopt and name a black baby out in some third world country. At the time you sent some money, to a charity organization and you received a photograph and a letter and an update on the under privileged kid you'd sponsored. This was around the late 60s, and Celtic's Lisbon Lions had lifted the European Cup a few years earlier so a lot of the kids chose Celtic players' names at the time for their new black brothers. So one of these days look out for a black African president of one of these small African nations called President Jimmy Johnstone. There must be thousands of these black kids out in Africa named after the Celtic team of the 60s. There's going to come a day when a Dr. Bobby Lennox of the Zianda University pops up on our T.V. screens talking about health care in Africa.

I started going to Rangers' games with all the Scarfers from around my way. There was only one Rangers' pub in our town so we had a right tight little mob.

We had a right battle with Celtic at the '81 Cup final at Hampden. We were proper Barmies. I then moved onto the Casual Scene, which was kicking in at the time up here. Barry Johnstone was the main player in the I.C.F. and we had a good strong firm.

I met Davey drinking in the town and soon became good friends. When we used to play Celtic there was a buzz going around the city the week before, and a few days before the game the phones would be red hot with who was meeting where and even the Scarfers would be up for it. People would be excited and well up for it. At one game over at Celtic Park, our mob met up in Duke Street and about 150 of us made our way over to the ground. At this particular game the Rangers' fans had to walk through the Celtic fans outside their end of the ground to get to the away fans' section. A lot of the Rangers' Barmies and Scarfers were getting attacked outside the stadium. Even kids were getting hit by these low life Celtic fans. We've come along just as all this is going on. There was hundreds of Celtic fans milling about and we give it to them. We fucking smashed them big time. We had two coppers with us, one that lashed out at anything that moved with his stick, and the other was a short sighted specky copper that couldn't see a thing. It was going off everywhere. They came across the road and were hitting our Scarfers unaware we were there. We moved in and surrounded their lot and hammered them. They got well fucked. It went on for about two miles and it was just none stop fighting. They threw everything at us but we never moved an inch. We put a show on that day.

Up near the Gallowgate, near the Cross, they mobbed up but were too sacred to come into us. One of the coppers, who had been trying to stop it, came over to us. "I tell ya what boys, you gave a good account of yaselves there," he said. "Cheers mate," one of our lot said. Two of our boys ended up in hospital but it was only to have a couple of stitches put in. Nothing too serious.

I rate Hibs as one of the best mobs. They've always been there, unlike Aberdeen who have another scummy mob who'd think nothing of hitting kids. They'd steal chocolate from a baby. They're another mob who sees drinking in a Glasgow pub miles from the ground as a result against us. They're another scruffy mob like Celtic.

I saw Celtic at Chelsea in a pre-season friendly and the Celtic boys that turned up looked like a mob of down and outs from Kings Cross. They're a rag tag bunch of dossers.

When I went out to watch Rangers in Belgium the first person we saw was a bloke in a Celtic shirt and I went up and asked him if he was drawing the dole out here. He looked at me blankly. I think he must have been Belgium. I think the Celtic idea of looking good at football is not wearing Stone Island or Prada. It's buying a suit at a car boot sale or wearing one of their dad's old cast off jumpers. They don't know the meaning of looking smart. When their boys got escorted down to the ground at Chelsea they were taking photos of the Chelsea firm being held back by the Old Bill. They've never seen fashion so looking smart's all new to them. They'd rather spend their dole on a bag of weed or on the brown stuff or a bottle of cider. The rest of football's all into Stone Island and the Celtic fans are more Clown Island. They're a bunch of muppets.

I now live down south and have changed my outlook on life. I realize now there's good and bad in all walks of life be it Catholic, Protestant, black or Asian. It takes al sorts to make a world but there's still only one team like Glasgow Rangers.

BROONEY

I'm originally from Airdrie, which is about 10 miles east of Glasgow. I first went to a Rangers' game when I was 6 and I think it was against St. Johnstone. I went with my old man who was a mad Rangers' fan. That was in the early 70s and I couldn't even tell you who was in the team in them days. I first started going after we'd just won the Cup Winners' Cup so the team was doing well. If I didn't go to games with my dad then my dad's mate would take me on a supporters' bus that went from the pub or the Orange Hall.

My area was 80% Rangers and even before the Casual scene started I can remember being about 13 or 14 and fighting with Hibs' fans. From there I got involved in gang fights with Catholic boys and then I got into the I.C.F. Two different firms from the East End and the South Side came together under the I.C.F. name. Some wanted to call the firm `Section Red` because that was the part of the ground where the boys used to meet up.

A few of the lads had been using the name H.M.S. (Her Majesty's Service) but then it got changed to the I.C.F. and that name stuck.

I started hanging around with the boys a couple of years after the I.C.F. had started and I knew Davie already. We met through a mutual friend and we've been pals ever since. I was never into the clubbing and the concerts and the music like him. I was too busy drinking. Over the years we've had some right battles with Celtic, even before the casual scene. At the Cup final in the 80s I saw guys getting hit over the head with full bottles of Pomainge. I think the reason why the Casual scene was slow to take off in Scotland was because basically people prefer their drink to buying designer clothes. It's as simple as that. That's the mentality of some people.

As the casual scene developed you had Rangers, Hibs and Aberdeen at the forefront of it. Teams like Dundee, Motherwell and Kilmarnock were never in the same league as us mob wise. They didn't do it week in week out. Airdrie's another game little mob but they couldn't live with the likes of us or Hibs. They just haven't got the numbers. Out of us, Hibs and Aberdeen we've all had our time at the top. One season we'd rule the roost and then Hibs would run the show for a couple of years, and then Aberdeen would come on strong and have a good firm. We've all been the top dogs at some time or another. Hooliganism in Scotland is still going strong although I haven't been up for a game for a few years.

I live down south now so I rarely get the chance to go to games. The last Rangers' game I went to was P.S.G. away in Paris. We held our own out there but it's a dodgy place to go to. I've also been to Bruges and Milan.

Over the years I've got to know many of Chelsea's main faces. A lot of them came up for one of the Scottish Cup finals a few years back, and I've kept in touch. Just a week after we met I was moving down to London and I met up with a few of the Chelsea lads on an anti I.R.A. march in London. There's a strong link between Chelsea and Rangers but a few of our boys follow Man City and a few follow Leeds.

When Celtic's Casuals first started they had a decent firm but their Casuals and their fans have never got on. The Celtic fans hated the

Celtic Casuals. They've even come to blows at times. The Celtic supporters once got battered by their own Casual firm, that's how stupid they all are. They've only got 30 or so Casuals now and they all dress like Big Issue sellers. You sometimes see them on I.R.A. parades and they look like the dregs of society. They'll turn out for their own parades but they wouldn't dare turn out for a Loyalist parade as there'd be too much of a backlash. They'd get smashed if they tried it.

We have a thing up in Scotland called Christmas Casuals. That's when someone who thinks they're a face gets a Stone Island jumper for Christmas and thinks because he's wearing it he's become one of the boys. We now have 30 or 40 youngsters coming through in a sort of new wave youth movement. For years there was no-one coming through but now I've been told there's new blood coming into the scene. I think the rave scene killed the original casual scene off but slowly and surely lots of the old faces are now making a comeback, both at Rangers and at Chelsea.

CHAPTER 3

Four times a year in Glasgow the city is filled with hate, passion, violence and a "must not lose" mentality. But this is no new situation. It's been going on for well over a hundred years. On one side of the city you have the blue of Rangers with its support coming from the Protestant community. Celtic, on the other hand, draws most of its support from the Catholic community with its links deep in Irish politics. Both clubs were founded in the 1880s within a few years of each other and at first they had a very close relationship with finances being the common bond.

In the late 1800s Celtic fans invaded the pitch in an effort to get the game abandoned against Rangers. At a Scottish Cup game in 1905 Celtic fans rioted and bought an end to the game as they trailed Rangers 2-0. Rival gangs helped stoke the flames of hatred between the two teams. All this was going on well before the outbreak of the First World War. Between the two wars there was trouble at almost every game between the teams with hundreds hurt and arrested.

Into the 50s and 60s trouble continued, with what was happening in Northern Ireland playing a major part at the old firm games. Officials from both sides even met with the police to discuss ways and to try and find solutions to the problem but many pointed the finger at religious sectarianism being the real reason behind the violence and the continuing hatred. But there again it didn't take a genius to work that one out. At one time it was suggested that if Celtic removed the Irish tricolour which flew at Parkhead and Rangers changed their policies on the signing of catholic players, and that meetings between the clubs were allowed to be attended by the media and the general public and that views were aired by both sides, out in the open, then things may at long last change. In two words, "no chance". No-one was prepared to give an inch.

From when I was born I've heard all about the differences. Pre-school age, Protestant and Catholic kids play in the streets and parks and live and play side by side quiet happily, but as soon as it's time to start school Protestant kids and other denominations are sent to one school and the Catholic kids are sent to Catholic only schools. So where's the sense in that? We all get on fine and then when you reach, say, 5 years old you're taught to dislike the children you've played with for years on the streets just because he or she's a different religion. How many kids that young could really tell you what religion means? Not many I bet. We'd all wear our Rangers scarves to school with pride and God forbid if there were any closet Celtic fans that rolled into school with a green and white scarf tied around their necks. They wouldn't have lasted a minute, let alone the rest of the day.

You do get Catholics supporting Rangers but I don't know too many Protestants that follow Celtic. Plus, you get a few boys from the Protestant side of things that have no real interest in the football but will turn up when we play Celtic just for the aggro. To me football's football. It's never been about religion, that's separate from football. The same with racism. Rangers' fans are portrayed as being racist, but again colour doesn't come into football. Aye there have been people outside Ibrox selling the right wing papers and some people do buy them and read them and we've not had that many black faces in our mob. We did have a half Chinese boy that went with us named Chinky Wilson and he was a good boy who was as game as fuck.

The first Celtic game I ever went to was about 1980 and it was the Scottish Cup Final played at Hampden Park. I was about 14 and my dad got me and my brother tickets but it was horrendous. Celtic scored a late winner in the final minute and at the end Celtic fans came onto the pitch to celebrate and one of them kicked an orange, plastic ball into the net and reeled away in mock celebrations. This was really taking the piss and Rangers' fans went onto the pitch for revenge. The two ends came on and half a dozen mounted police tried to separate the warring mobs. Bricks, bottles, stones, cans and lumps of wood rained down on the pitch from the terraces. People were throwing bottles from the back of the Rangers' terraces and they weren't reaching the pitch and were hitting our own supporters standing at the front. In them days people could take drinks into the game and most people took a carry out from the pub. This trouble must have gone on for nearly an hour and the final outcome was over 200 fans arrested inside and outside the stadium. Outside there were more running battles. The press said the next day that it was the worst trouble in 70 years at Hampden. The game had been on television and the clubs pointed the finger of blame on one another. Some members of the press even went as far as saying that the blame lay at Rangers' door citing the old chestnut that if Rangers were to sign catholic players then things like this would never happen. Others blamed the Celtic players and fans for their wild celebrations, and others blamed drink. There were even calls to ban the clubs from entering the competition the following season.

When I got home dad asked me if I'd seen the trouble. "No I replied, I was well out of it" but in reality I was glued to it. For years my dad kept me away from the Rangers and Celtic games because in 1971 at a New Year's Day game a friend of his had died. Rangers were losing this particular game and hundreds of fans had seen enough and headed for the exits but with a minute to go Rangers equalized. Lots of those leaving heard the goal celebrations and turned and headed back into the ground. It seems that a couple of fans stumbled on the steep steps and hundreds went down like a deck of cards and with it in the crush the metal crash barriers down the middle bent and mangled under the weight of bodies. Tragically, 33 fans sadly lost their lives with a further 500 injured.

The casual scene for both clubs started in the early 80s. Aberdeen, Hibs and Motherwell claim to have led the way in Scotland with some Aberdeen fans claiming they got the idea after a European game down at Liverpool, and the Scousers also claim that they were the originators of the casual dress fashion look. I disagree with that completely. The Scousers reckon they started it around 1977 after their European Cup Final in Rome and that their Scallys went on the rob and came home with the latest designs. Total bollocks. Talk to any of the London teams and their fans were always years ahead on terrace fashion. The original Skinhead look of the late 60s and early 70s was London born. Wasn't the original Skinheads the first casuals with the Harrington jackets, Ben Shermans, Sta-prest, loafers, Cromies, pork pie hats, and then came the Suedehead look with the slightly longer hair, the Rupert the Bear check loud trousers, the Jazzy, loud shirts and the fringe and Buckle loafers. Jonathan King under the name of the Piglets done the song Johnny Reggae in 1971 which was about the Suedehead look of the time. Then came the punk scene, all born in London and then the Sports look of tennis and golf players, again all born in the south. Talk to any of the older lads from Chelsea and they'll tell you of having their best gear nicked on trips up to Liverpool in the 60s and 70s and they'll tell you the Scousers were years behind the dress stakes in their donkey jackets and Dunlop green flash trainers. Original Casuals? I don't think so. Thieving cunts? Yes, your number 1, but originators of fashion? No fucking chance. There, that's my views and I'm sticking to them.

Celtic's mob in the early days ran the city centre. They seemed to be in all the pubs and knew most of the doormen. I remember once I was in a pub and a few of Celtic's main faces that I knew were in there. One lad who was in their company and was a bit of a clown wouldn't leave me alone and was trying to give me some mouth. I just ignored him and let him gob off. He went off to the fruit machine and pumped some money in. I came up next to him, took my dick out of my trousers and pissed all down his leg. I zipped myself back up and went and sat back down with the bird I was with. This clown comes over and throws a drink over the girl and me but most of it went over her and she points out that the stuff in the glass was warm and she reckoned it was piss. I called my mate, Sean, over and asked him to find out what had gone on. He went away and came back and told me he'd found out the cunt had pissed in a glass and had thrown it over us. He told me not to do anything about it in there as the place was full of Celtic boys and the whole place would go up if I touched him. The bloke walked past me grinning so I asked him if I could have a word in the toilet. He asked me if I thought he was daft and with that I cracked him and splattered his nose across his face. The place was in uproar but I knew a lot of the main faces and the rest of them just didn't have the bottle to have a go at me.

Celtic at the time could roughly pull the same numbers as us and it was guaranteed there'd be running battles with them every weekend in the town centre. If we were playing away they'd wait on us and if they were away we'd wait for their return. It was tit for tat. It didn't matter where they was or how late they arrived back, we would wait.

Back in the early days Id say it was honours even with them coming out on top in one battle and the following week we'd smash them, but over the course of time we got our act together and stayed on top of them. I think the one row that did swing it our way was when they had a big do on in a local night club and they had boys up from Wrexham and were putting a bit of a show on for their guests. I walked in and you could cut the atmosphere with a knife. Word soon got around amongst our lot just where Celtic's mob and their guests were. At 3 o'clock in the morning we had 150 boys out waiting for them around the corner from the club in George Square. There were lines of police outside the club and in the end they had to hold us back and escort the Celtic firm away from the area. It was all their main boys and from that night things changed and they knew it. Some of our lot were breaking through their police escort and punching them and fucking off before they got nicked. When we played them at their place, we even thought about taking the battle to them by going into their end which was called The Jungle but we'd have needed our full quota of our men to do that. Plus we'd have got sussed out straight away because we'd be the only ones not decked out in green and white.

We were playing Motherwell away and our game was cancelled and we had 120 boys in a mob so we decided to head over to Parkhead where Celtic were playing Hamilton. We went in and stood on the terraces next to the Jungle, which is full of the home supporters. It wasn't long before punches were thrown and the sound of The Sash being sung echoed across Parkhead. The police moved in and escorted us down to the other end of the ground where the Hamilton fans were stood, who, by the way, were looking a bit bewildered by it all. There was thirty odd thousand fans howling and booing us. A few of our lot unfolded big Union Jack flags and you could see the steam coming from three sides of the ground. They were fucking steaming mad that we had the audacity to pull off something like this. We, on the other hand, were over the moon that everything had gone to plan and we'd upset our biggest rivals and humiliated them on their own patch.

Things like this would never ever happen when we play one another. For one thing all games between us are all ticket and tickets are like gold dust, and secondly the police have almost everything sewn up, on a match day Celtic would rarely come to Ibrox in an organized mob. You'd get all the usual pissed up, mouthy; beer monsters all dressed up in their green and white, singing their rebel songs, but no firm of boys.

One game they did turn up about 300 handed and 70 of us met them in the middle of the street and it was a right toe to toe until the police broke it up. Usually the games are well segregated with their supporters coming in from one side of the stadium and ours coming in from another way. You do get the odd scuffle but it's quickly broken up by the police who stand no nonsense and deal with incidents very firmly to say the least. There's a 5 or 6 mile distance between the two stadiums so there's plenty of bars and pubs where the boys from each side can meet and organize a row. A couple of times their mob's turned up at Ibrox while the game's been going on and they'll phone us on the mobiles and tell us they're here, but it's all bollocks and they're just normally trying to make a name for themselves.

Aberdeen are another firm who always turn up with a police escort and who never seem to want to go it alone when they visit Ibrox. Come to think of it I don't think they've ever met us once on their own. Before the days of mobile phones and computers it was amazing how many times we bumped into Celtic's firm and it was mostly down to sheer chance. But I do rate their mob. I can't take the fact away they are game and I'll give credit where credit's due. They have a lot of good boys. They have about 15 or 20 boys who come over from Ireland who are as game as fuck. They come from Boheimians or somewhere like that. There are hundreds of fans that follow Celtic or Rangers who come across on the buses but hardly any of them are hard core casuals. They're just mostly normal supporters who talk a good fight or who come across to play in their flute bands. But to me the greatest flute player of all time was Gazza. Him playing his imaginary flute at a game made him an instant hero amongst the Rangers' fans. I had the pleasure of meeting him up at Loch Lomond and he was brilliant, a real gentleman. I had a good chat with him and I'd put him right up there with Graham Roberts, Andy Goram and Davie Cooper. They were all committed on the park and Rangers through and through. I had that picture of him playing his flute on my mobile phone and I'd send it to my Celtic mates just to wind them up but the biggest wind up between the two sets of fans is the songs aimed at one another.

The Sash is one such song which sends them mad. It's basically about the Battle of the Boyne in 1690 and the Celtic fans hate it and respond with their I.R.A. songs. God Save the Queen and Rule Britannia and The Billy Boys song is just a few which we sing to them. The Billy Boys song is based on Billy Fullerton who led the Bridgeton Billy Boys gang in the mid 1920s and was one of the most feared gangs ever to walk the streets of Glasgow. Apparently the gang first formed when Billy was playing in a local football match and he scored the winning goal. One of the opposing team took great exception to this and attacked Billy boy with a hammer. The story goes that he rounded up nearly a thousand men and from that day on terrorized the Catholic community. With Rangers it's a real strong pro British/English link, but with Celtic it's the opposite with an almost hatred of all things British/English. They are very much pro I.R.A/Irish/Sin Fein and it comes across in the songs they sing. The Soldier Song which is against the crown and pro I.R.A. seems to be one of their favourites. Now such songs are outlawed and sectarian songs and the singing of them is an offence. Fines and even jail are now the penalty.

My local pub's a Celtic pub and when we beat them 3-0, I was up on the table singing and celebrating with an England top on. A lot of them don't like it. My pals in the pub just laugh. Nowadays at the old firm games the two sets of fans try to out shout one another and try to sing one another to death. Also the size of the two mobs has dwindled drastically. Against us now all they can maybe muster is say 40 to 50 faces and we could raise anything from 70 to 100 so the size of the mobs has decreased over the years. The Celtic Casuals were disliked by their own supporters who on more than one occasion turned on them and let it be known they weren't welcome at Celtic games. I heard one story where their Casuals were at an away game and were drinking in a pub. A mob of Celtic beer monsters walked past and someone noticed the casuals drinking inside. The beer monsters laid siege to the pub and terrorized the Casuals trapped inside. There is no love lost between the two factions.

The last real bit of trouble between them and us happened not at Ibrox or Parkhead, but on the Troon to Larne Ferry. Rival supporters clashed on their return journey to Northern Ireland and the reports in the media claimed that over 100 people were involved and that the riot police, in full battle dress, had to board the ship to restore order, which by all accounts took quite a while. But when people get seriously injured or lose their lives in the name of football and all because they support a different team, then things have gone too far. There have been in the past fatalities and serious injuries on both sides. A Celtic lad at one game was chased near Ibrox by Rangers fans and was thrown off one of the walkways over the motorway. He suffered serious brain damage and the boy was only 22 or 23 years old. Another boy was chased in the city centre after a fight and died on the steps of the sheriff's court after one of our lot stabbed him. Arrests were made and a couple of the boys were put away for it. All this happened a few years ago now but it's still so sad. This isn't football, it's too much.

One of the best rows I ever witnessed with them lot was when about 40 of us were walking down towards Parkhead and as we passed an Irish bar the doors burst open and a mob came out well tooled up. One bloke was swinging a hammer around. I nutted a bloke and we backed off. The Celtic mob had grabbed a bloke in the melee and were punching fuck out of him. They had him on the floor but we couldn't do a thing because we were out numbered and they were well tooled up. As I said, one of them's grabbed him and dragged him up the road and as he's being dragged along his jacket's rose up to his chest and underneath he had on a Celtic shirt. Brilliant! We pissed ourselves laughing when we realized they've given one of their own a good leathering. They bashed the fuck out of him.

At times we'd meet early on London Road when we had them at their place and after a few hours' people would be out of their nuts on the booze, puff or Charlie, or all three with some people. A few people would carry weapons and the police were very disorganized. Unless they stumbled across us we'd do as we wanted and then once we'd left the pub then the uniform police would escort us to the ground. The horses and dogs would be bought in along with other support units.

One time we came out of a pub in Duke Street and came along near the Celtic end of the ground. 60 or 70 of us got to the crossroads near the ground. We had no Old Bill with us and it was about half an hour before kick off so there were thousands of them all around us, and then it went. They came into us from every angle and we never budged. I got cut under the chin by some boy flashing a knife. The

Celtic mob had earlier taken some right liberties with some of our supporters and they'd been seen hitting normal blokes with shirts on and hitting blokes who were with their wives or girlfriends. One of the Rangers fanzines, even wrote an article about our fight outside the Celtic end and basically said we were fighting for all Rangers' fans that day after the Celtic fans had taken unprecedented liberties with lots of Rangers' fans, who were doing no more than peacefully walking towards the stadium. We were eventually rounded up by the police and at the height of the fighting a police horse came around the corner at quiet a speed and skidded and nearly went down on all fours. The copper on board had the right hump. They eventually pushed us up a side street and surrounded us until they got in the support units. Those of us with tickets were taken to the other end of the ground under the watchful eye of a police helicopter hovering overhead. A lot of us without tickets were taken away from the stadium and ended up in a pub in the town centre where we met up with the rest of the boys after the game.

I've been nicked a few times at old firm games and gone to court and received fines, but I never really bothered going into the Celtic games. It was all about turning up, showing your face and doing a bit. To some people Celtic v Rangers was more than football and to some people it still is. One of the best moments against them was when we played them one St Patrick's Day. Celtic's mob was drinking in `The Nobody's Inn` and we heard where they were. 30 of us came from one direction and another 30 came from the other way and charged through the doors. As we burst in one of them's holding a big cake with candles on it. That went up in the air and the majority of them have headed for the toilet door but because they can only get through one at a time there's a bit of a snarl up. They were getting punched and kicked up the arse as panic set in. We just took the piss. Suddenly some old boy, obviously a Celtic fan, has jumped on my back and won't let go. I'm trying to shake him off but he wouldn't let go. I carried him outside and he still clung on and in the end a few of the boys got him off and sent the silly old bastard on his way. The pub was Charlie Nicholas's old pub but I've never heard him recall that story. He wasn't there that day. Well, I never saw him. Perhaps the old boy on my back had the hump because it was his birthday cake that went up in the air?

Not long ago we came across a group of the Celtic players in town all suited and booted on their way to some do. The lads have spotted them and gone straight into them and after a few punches have chased them up the road. All but one of them stood and without naming names this ex Norwich player stood and exchanged punches and the boys said fair play to him, he's the only one out of the lot of them that stood, and he was as game as fuck and they now have total respect for him. We went into The Finnigan's Wake, which is an Irish pub and where a few of their boys drink. We met up in there in twos and threes and they were all standing around singing their rebel songs, and then it's kicked off. A few of their boys got cut as the place got smashed up. They have in the past attacked a couple of our pubs and they've turned up at Annie Millers, bar a few times. That's, why there's quite a few bars around Glasgow with the windows removed or boarded up already. Prevention being better than a cure.

You can tell a Celtic fan a mile off. They have got some dressers but they've also got a few scruffy bastards that look like beggars. You know, a half empty beer can in one hand, a mop of curly or ginger hair that ain't seen a comb or brush for months or even years, their trouser flies undone with their stained string pants poking through, their shirts and jackets not done up right so the buttons and button holes don't match up. They have the look of someone that's slept rough for a while. Also, when they have something to smile about, like their Giro finally arriving, then they reveal missing or black front teeth. And the men look even worse.

BILLY BRITAIN

I started going when I was about 6 with my older brother to Rangers. I'm now 34 so I've been going a good few years.

My first ever game was Rangers v Clyde. Clyde used to play in the Gorbals area of Glasgow. Gordon Smith, Bobby Russell, Derek Johnstone, John Gregg, who was then coming to the end of his career, were in that Rangers team.

My brother was Rangers daft. He used to follow them everywhere. He would come back home from games and tell me all sorts of stories.

My first memory of seeing any violence at a game was the 1980 Cup Final. Celtic beat us 1-0 in extra time. My brother was at the game and after Celtic scored that late winner, Rangers' fans came pouring onto the pitch. Celtic fans joined them and there was a mass battle with horses charging across the pitch and with bottles flying through the air. This is all live on T.V. I was frightened watching it but at the same time it excited me. I was only about 8 but I was loving it in a strange sort of way. I was intrigued by it all and maybe that's what got me hooked.

I was from the East end of Glasgow and was a bit of a scally. I was a wee thief. I liked going shop lifting but I soon got into the fighting side of football. There was a bit of a football gang culture amongst us youngens. We were called the Rangers Soccer Babes and we'd fight most nights with our rivals, The Celtic Soccer Babes. We were mostly all young Rangers boys but we had one or two Celtic fans that were converted and came over to our side. They'd come up to our area around Duke Street or we'd go over to them and meet in the town.

Some nights there'd be 50 or 60 aside. It was mental. We were mostly 13 or 14 years old with a few youngsters thrown in. I'd sometimes go to an under 18 club called `Henry Africa's` and we'd fight with Celtics' young Casual mob. We had one of the Rangers' older boys working the door so he looked out for us. That was about '87 and I've never got the casual scene out of my system.

In the beginning the first guys I met in the Casual scene were Marky and Mulligan who came from Possal Park, which is a big tough area. I remember we went through to Hibs at Easter Road one Christmas and Marky had a Santa suit on and he ended up in the jail.

In my opinion, and I've seen some top boys at Rangers, the top three were Barry Johnstone, Davie and a boy called Harky. I've seen hundreds of guys who were as game as fuck but as I say, in my opinion these guys stick out in my mind above all the rest. I'd look up to them three without a doubt. They all had a massive influence on me. My brother turned to heroin as he got older and my father left the house when I was 5 so Harky was a bit of a father figure to me. He was really good to me when I was younger and he helped shape my life. He showed me some morals, taught me respect and not to mug everyone off, and to fuck people about. "Don't be a prick and enjoy life" he told me, and I listened. "In fear front people out, tell the truth and show no fear."

I'm only a wee cunt but I won't back down. I'll have a go. I think I'm well respected in the Rangers' firm but that's not for me to say. People can make their own minds up about me. Faces in other mobs know who I am and some bad mouth me, but they don't have a lot to say when I'm chasing them up the street, the pricks. My view of the Rangers, Celtic thing is that they've only had a good mob for one season and that was a really good mob.

I had to go to the thing we have up here called The Juvenile Panel, which is a court for under 16s. I got nicked for fighting with the Celtic Casuals and I had a cut eye and my hair all over the place as I stood in front of the bench. Them days Celtic had some good boys like Irish Joe and Stu Campbell. I got fucked by about 30 of them trying to be a big hard man.

There's been some good mobs up here and on their day Aberdeen and Motherwell ain't too bad, but you'd have to put Hibs up there above them.

The first time I heard the word casual to describe a football mob was after Motherwell played Aberdeen at Firs Park. That must have been around '83 or '84. Dundee on their day can pull a good sized mob and every so often you'll get a wee team up here pull a good mob for a couple of seasons. Someone like Falkirk or Airdrie will surprise people and turn out and be as game as fuck.

The thing is at Rangers we could always pull good numbers but we had a hard core of front liners and the rest were what we called Christmas Casuals or Dressers. They wouldn't throw a punch and would fuck off if it came on top and you'd find them back in the pub boasting about what they'd done, whereas in reality they'd done fuck all.

The only time I've feared for my safety is when we had that planned meet with Hibs. We got off the train at Slateford, which is about 3 mile outside of Edinburgh, and we found ourselves on an industrial estate and we got fucked. There was only about 20 of us and some of our boys were stabbed and others got well battered. I've never been so glad to see a policeman as I could run no more, my legs had gone. Psychologically that day done my head in. I was really concerned for my own safety.

The next time we went through to Easter Road we took a massive mob and Hibs wouldn't come out of the pub. We were well up for it that day and they shit themselves. We wanted revenge.

We'd regularly go through to Edinburgh with 400 boys. The thing was there was a power struggle within our ranks. The East-end boys didn't sometimes get on with the Northend boys and sometimes there'd be fights amongst our own firm. Week in Week out it was the same faces. We've had some good boys.

A few years ago there was calls from the press up here and down south to allow Rangers and Celtic to play in the English Premiership. Celtic's fans would have been all right because they're what we call scarf swappers. But we'd have been lucky to have lasted one season. Most teams would have welcomed Celtic with open arms but this is a support that sings songs about bombing English cities and glorifies political violence, whereas Rangers must be the most pro British club there is. When you go to Ibrox all you'll see is Union Jack flags and fans with England shirts on. In the 70s the bulk of the Scotland's team support came from Rangers. Now it's been hijacked by the Tartan Tadgers with their kilts and their long ginger beards.

At Rangers we'd been a sleeping giant for 10 years until Souness came in with plenty of money and we bought the best English players and it turned our fortunes around. We were one of the biggest clubs in the world in terms of support, and money. We were bigger than Man Utd. We were up there with the likes of the Turkish team, Galatasary, who have millions of fans, and the likes of Spanish sides Barcelona and Real Madrid. We would compete in the transfer market with AC. Milan and Inter and Juventus.

Celtic have never been able to do that. Just recently we took fourteen thousand down to Derby for a Testimonial. It's only the police panicking about our huge numbers that causes trouble like when we played Man Utd and the police closed the whole town. Talk about over reacting. What was that all about? When we played them up here I was on two charges and ready to go to court. On that day Man Utd it was said, took their biggest away mob ever up here and in a way they took the piss. But outside the ground 20 of our lot didn't budge an inch. We tried to get into the town and have it with them after the game but there was police everywhere and we were just jail bait. We heard for the game at Old Trafford they had a 700 strong mob waiting for us at a pub near the ground. They'd heard there was four thousand Rangers' fans down for the game and that we'd be arriving on mass. They knew where we were drinking but there was just too many Old Bill for anything to happen. Also, tickets for us were scarce for that game. We didn't get a very big allocation so tickets were fetching up to £300 a time. The hard core blue noses couldn't afford them so the trendies and the rich and famous jumped on the bandwagon and snapped them up at any price. Both them games against United were total balls up, on our part. But I guarantee it would be different if we met again.

CHAPTER 4

THE FUTURE'S ORANGE

Being a good Protestant boy, I've had a few run ins with the other side. Besides the name calling, we call them "Taigs" or "Fenians" and they call us a whole host of choice names, but it's when the threats start that you have to deal with it one way or another.

A mate of mine went into the local Orange Lodge for a drink and three Irish fellas have seen him and asked if they could have a word in private. They asked him "do you know Davie Carrick"? He looked at them blankly. It turns out a few bar owners from the Catholic side were sick of having their pubs smashed up by our boys and had called in these Irish lads to mediate a peace deal. The bottom line was we were driving their customers away. It's funny how the two sides can come together when it's about business and making money and how money can bridge the gap between the great religious divide.

My name also appeared in an I.R.A. approved magazine called Chocey Ala, which translates as "Our Day Will Come". It's a

Republican propaganda magazine and they printed me and me mate Sandy's names. See what it was basically saying was that Sandy and me were racist thugs that were members of the B.N.P., which was total bollocks. Some boys from the Celtic Casuals had obviously put our names in the frame. My missus was at work doing a night shift and a bloke that worked with her came up to her and handed her the magazine, which was folded on the page where my name and address was highlighted. She was well upset and wanted to know what was going on. We found out who'd done it and before I found him he went and apologized to my brother. Sandy went and saw a bloke he knew that had close links with the I.R.A. And he re-assured Sandy that it would never happen again and he apologized. This certain bloke at the time did a lot of fund raising for the I.R.A. but a few years back he died, but still we never ever got any more shit so the bloke was true to his word.

Not just in Glasgow but all over Great Britain Orange Lodges can be found. But I've never shown any interest in becoming a member. In every Lodge is a picture of the Queen, on the wall and on entering the Lodge anybody wearing a cap or a hat has to remove it in respect for the Queen. That's about all I really know about Orange Lodges. I suppose they're a bit like the Freemasons or a social club, with a few well-chosen members. I honestly don't know how things work inside these places but I know most of them have no windows and they ain't exactly the best surroundings to spend time in. But that's my choice and my opinion.

The Catholics have their version, which is The Knights of St. Columbus and I suppose it's run along the same lines as the Orange Lodges but I don't think you'll find many folk in Rangers tops having a drink and passing the time of day in them.

The political marches in Glasgow are another place where the two sides cross paths. Well, not just in Glasgow but the I.C.F. have traveled to Edinburgh to oppose Republican marches. The Bloody Sunday marches and the James Connolly Parades are two events where you'll find our boys out on the streets. The Celtic Casuals used to do the security on the Republican marches in Glasgow so we'd set out to attack their security boys and the marchers. There'd be anything up to 500 people on these marches, many wearing Celtic shirts. Many of the marchers would come from the predominately Catholic areas of Royston and Brigton and others would come from further afield, such as across from Northern Ireland and up from London. Most Orange Lodges will have a flute band and the marching season starts about May and goes right through the summer months. The marches usually go from one Lodge to another Lodge or from a Lodge to a local park where there'd be a picnic and a few drinks and then they'd march back again.

Most Lodges have a Union Jack flying above it, hence the name Loyalists. Being an Orangeman means being loyal to one's Queen and country. I'll let my good mate, Colin Bell, tell you more about Orangemen, Loyalists, Rangers and the U.D.A.

"My name's Colin Bell and I'm 35 years old and I've been watching Glasgow Rangers since I was 14. All my family are, Rangers' fans so it's in the blood. I seriously hate them Republicans. You'd never catch me socializing with any of them Celtic bastards. I'm more into the political side of things, then the football. Everybody I know that went to Rangers had a passion about the team and a passion about their beliefs.

In the early days of the I.C.F. we done a fund raising dance at, `The Bristol` pub and raised over fifteen hundred pound which went into a central fund in case any of the boys got nicked, and needed a few quid, but in the end the money went to Loyalist prisoners' wives in

Northern Ireland. Which to me is a far better cause. To me Rangers and politics go hand in hand. I was in the Orange Order when I was younger. I didnee agree with the ethics of what they done or, more to the point, what they've never done. In my eyes I feel they should do more for the paramilitary side of things. But then my beliefs on that front have always got me in trouble.

I've visited Northern Ireland 22 times in one year. The authorities have also stopped me so many times because in their words "I was a known face". It didn't matter if I flew or went by boat, I'd get stopped, searched and quizzed by Special Branch. It didn't need a genius to work out that I was a face because I'd done a 5 year jail sentence for gun running. I'd been caught with six guns after being set up by a U.D.A. Brigadier who was a grass and an informer.

At one time I could go to Northern Ireland and walk through the Shankhill and be treated with the utmost respect, but not any more. That's because of the split within the U.D.A. The U.D.A. was once a legal organization but now it's been outlawed and has been made an illegal organization. The whole thing is now riddled with grasses and informers and it's completely lost its ways in what it once stood for. I could have gone anywhere over there and no cunt would bother me. My good mate, Johnny Adair, has suffered the same fate with informers, wrong 'uns and grasses turning on him. When he was banged up in prison I'd visit him every other week. There's been a lot of infighting within our ranks. It's been a dirty war with lots of infiltration. Throughout all this I've still stayed loyal to Johnny Adair. I'm still great friends with him and if I needed him he'd be there for me. He's a true friend.

I was only 21 years old when I got my 5 year jail sentence and I was well set up. I had a gut feeling it was going to go Pete Tong but if I'd have done a runner and fucked off and not seen it through, I'd have been looked upon as a right shit bag. Principles made me stick to my task. I'm no coward and I've proved that. Not like the cunt who ordered that I be murdered, all this after Id been caught, and the order to get me and kill me as been given three times. An active service unit was dispatched to sort me out. I know this as fact because the flute band I associated with was told to stay away from me. I was drinking in a club in East Belfast after I'd missed my flight from Aldergrove Airport to Glasgow. I was sitting drinking with my mate's Dad and I was just pouring a bottle of drink into a glass when the cunts have grabbed me. I turned around and waved the bottle in their faces as they backed off. The barman has hit the panic button behind the bar and the four or five blokes that come for me fucked off. They were just following orders from above and there was no way they'd have shot me inside that club. I grabbed my mate's Dad and got out of there.

The rumour going around at the time was I was out of Belfast that night, a bit rapid but that's bollocks. I stayed another night before heading back to Glasgow. They've come for me since but I've not been there. After all I've done for the cause they still wanted to take me out.

Another incident that don't add up was when we were returning from a trip to Belfast and were due to come back on the Sea Cat but for some reason it was cancelled so we switched to come back by boat, which we caught with minutes to spare. I never drink on the one and a half- hour crossing because I like to keep a clear head knowing I'm going to get shit from the Special Branch when we dock at the other end. The boat was near on empty as it was a Sunday night so we went up to the back of the boat where there's a designated area for smokers. This bloke about 6ft 2" comes up behind us and says to my mate's girlfriend "your boyfriend's an arsehole". Next thing he's started arguing with me and does me in the face with a full bottle of Budweiser. I was out on my feet. I was out cold. I was knocked out as my brain went forward and hit my skull. Apparently a doctor bought me back to life and saved me. When I was in the back of an ambulance I was charged but they didn't take me to hospital, they took me to a police station and tried to question me before I was taken to hospital.

In hospital no-one was allowed to see me and I was put on a drip. I pulled the drip out and discharged myself and phoned a taxi to take me to another hospital but a copper turns up in an unmarked car to pick me up. My mate, who was with me, twigged it straight away. In the end I went to hospital in Glasgow where it was discovered after a scan, that I had 3 blood clots and minor brain damage. The bloke that done the assault went to court and got fuck all. I thought he'd get a G.B.H. or something or even two years. The reason he got off light was because I believe he was an undercover policeman. Just like his mate, the undercover cab driver. Things just didn't add up and they still don't. There's more evidence to suggest I'm right and I know I'm right so we'll leave it at that.

Rangers were playing Aberdeen and me and another boy nipped across to Belfast for the weekend. That weekend there'd been a funeral for some Republican who Sinn Fein had fought for nearly 40 odd years to have his body exhumed. It turned out the funeral was as big as the Bobby Sands one. As we're queuing to get on the boat three blokes kept looking at me and I stared back at them. "What you looking at you prick"? I said. Four other blokes came over and stood next to them. "What you looking at"? I asked again. "Nothing" one of them replied. "That's all right then" I said, and I booked in and went through the metal detector and because I went on across on the boat that often, I knew most of the staff at the port. I was on first name terms with a lot of them. "Are you off ya head"? One of them asked and she explained that there were 300 Republicans booked on our crossing. Then I saw all their drums and all their musical instruments being carried on board. Once on we headed for the fruit machine at the back of the boat. All eyes were on us as we walked through the crowded deck. At the end of the day I knew they wouldn't try anything because the place was all camerad up, but that didn't stop a few of them barging into me as I passed. I bounced off quite a few of them but I gave as good as I got. I put some money into the fruit machine and a bloke about 6ft 6" came and played the machine next to me. "Bell, I hope every one's a loser" he said as I pumped my pound coins into the machine. He didn't look at me and carried on playing. "Oh aye I said, the boat's full of losers". I could almost smell the shit oozing out of my mate's arse. We left the fruities and headed for the bar. There's a cunt sat there and he pulls out a belt. "When this boat docks at the other end you're getting this buckle around your head" he says, and my reply to that was "when this boat docks I'll strangle you with the fucking belt". As I stood at the bar, waiting to order a drink coins were landing at my feet. I bent down, picked them up and threw them back in the direction they'd just come from. They were just trying to goad me into a fight, as they stood there staring at us "I've had enough of this" I said to my mate, I'm going to the toilet and if I'm not out in 5 minutes come in and see what's going on". I'm thinking if I'm going to get it then I might as well do my best out of the way of the cameras. I'm standing at the urinals having piss and a couple of them came in but didn't say a word. "You're all Fannys man" I said aloud, zipped myself up and walked out. They will never had a better chance in their lives to have a go at me but they wouldn't touch me or come near me.

The boat docked and me and me mate stood out on the balcony outside looking down onto the port and you could cut the atmosphere with a knife. At one stage the captain had sent a message down through one of the crew that if I wanted to I could go up and sit with him. I declined his offer. The only chance now these thick cunts had of having a go at me was on one of the staircases as we got off and I told my mate this. As everyone began to disembark we made our way off and followed the crowds. Then this wee cow turns around and accuses me of spitting in her face. I denied it because I hadn't it was as simple as that. "Oi Bell, you're only hard when you're in a crowd" I heard a voice from behind me snarl and with that one of them's hit me up the side of the head, and with that some other cunts cracked me from the other side. I remember thinking "stay on your feet, don't go down". My head's spinning and I'm surrounded by a baying mob. My mate's gone missing, and then I go into action with arms and fists going like a windmill. I back them off; I put my head down and go for it. All of a sudden a doorway appears in front of me, and I managed to pull myself though to the other side and they tried to follow but it was like a cartoon with dozens of guys trying to squeeze through the opening at the same time but all they did was get stuck. "You fucking simple bastards" I shouted, and I was going bang, bang and was giving it to them. It went on for ages as I picked my punches. It took the Special Branch 40 minutes to come on board and stop the fighting. There was just one arrest and yes, you've guessed it. That was me, I was arrested, strip searched and released without charge. My sister came down with my brother-in-law in their B.M.W. to pick me up but before I went I smashed one of the bastard's motors up with a baseball bat and told another one of them to tell the rest of the cunts that "Colin done that".

One of Celtic's top boys who wasn't even on the boat, told me if I left him alone he would give me the names and addresses of those involved on the boat. He was out to save his own neck. I was told that if I stayed away from him he'd get me their phone numbers. He's dead now, nothing to do with what went on but he's no longer with us I'm told.

Many people may see my views as extreme, but everybody has their own limits. Some people are good at organizing, some at fund raising; some are good at military planning. Not being big headed but from a young age I was good at all of them. My beliefs are still as strong now as they've ever been. That's why I moved away from the Orange Order. I know the Orangemen apprentice boys and the Paramilitaries are all loyalists at heart but it's up to the individual how far they are prepared to take their beliefs. The same thing with politics and being in the mob at Rangers. One thing's for certain, I'd never run or hide from trouble when it came".

CHAPTER 5

THE CASUALS

As a casual firm Rangers were behind Motherwell, Hibs and Aberdeen in the terms of getting our act together. We'd always take thousands to away games but generally relied on pure numbers to crush any opposition. But with the birth of our own I.C.F. that all changed. Hibs, since the casual scene started in Scotland, have given Rangers the most grief. Edinburgh is only 45 minutes from Glasgow so there's no great distance between the teams. One time they were easily the best firm in Scotland and could pull numbers of anything up to 6-700. At one time they even had a couple of women on their front line. They had a good firm that's for sure.

Edinburgh is nowhere near as rough a city as Glasgow. We'd out-do them when it comes to the gangster types and the rough estates and the schemes, but they could pull a decent mob for the football, or fittba, as they say. A lot of their boys came from around the Leith area of Edinburgh. They were all dressers as well and most of them had all the latest gear so they were well up on all the latest fashions.

On one occasion we were playing them at Easter Road and arranged to meet them on the edge of Edinburgh at Slateford. There was only about 25 of us on the train and then we got a call from one of our boys, Warren. He told us that Hibs were waiting on us and had a good 100 boys in a mob, apparently it was one of the best firms they'd put together for years and the 100 they had out this day were all their top boys. He advised us to stay on the train and carry on through. Out of our mob on the train I probably only knew 8 or 9 and the rest were just idiots who were along for the ride. One of ours had a bag with brick hammers in and they were quickly handed out.

We were meeting in the middle of nowhere and it was odds on Hibs would be tooled up. We got off at Slateford Road and within seconds a full road of them came into view. We didn't hold back and went straight into them. We've thought so fuck it, we went for it but we got wiped out and as fighting went on all over the road five of us got split up, and we backed off. One of our boys held them off with a bottle of squirt but by their sheer weight of numbers they ran us up the road. They had one of our lot down on the ground and were kicking the fuck out of him. "Hey boys, one shouted, are you not coming back for ya wee pal"? Our boy was unconscious and one of them lifted his head up and smashed him with one of them big heavy glass ashtrays. It was fucking horrible so it was. In the end they've come across the road at an angle to us and we've somehow ended up right in amongst them. They got squirted and backed off and that's what saved us that day.

There was a big inquiry into where the rest of our firm was that day but it was the time of the Raves and the Acid Scene and lots of our lot were into all the peace and love and Es and all that shit. Peace and love ain't no good to ya when you've got over a hundred Hibs C.C.S. Casuals baying for your blood and wanting to cut ya balls off. The

Hibs Capital City Service definitely won that battle and in reality it took a few years to get our revenge.

The next time we went through I had a chat with my mate, Big James McLeod, who was one of their main boys, and it's a funny thing we ended up being good mates. I told him we were coming and he said a few of their boys were in jail and they now didn't have the numbers. "Nor did we" I said, when 25 of us turned up at your place". He was there that day we got battered and he even said he couldn't believe it when a handful of us steamed straight into their boys.

That same season when we played them at Ibrox we had a good tight firm of about 70 or 80 that turned out and it was a nasty mob who were well up for it. But Hibs didn't show. One of the boys took me to one side and asked if he could have a quiet word, we went to his car parked outside. He lifted the boot up and lying there were two sawn off shotguns. I'll use one, he said proudly, and I'm looking for someone to use the other one".

"That's nothing to do with football" I told him. He's no longer with us as he got shot and died a few years back. Nothing to do with football, it was drugs related.

When we next played them again at Easter Road I had a chat with one of their boys on the mobile phone and 80 of our firm went through there. Nothing happened before the game but I could see their boys in the crowd inside the ground, but we couldn't get at one another. After the game as we made our way out onto the street I got a call on the mobile to meet them at The Bridges which is up at the St. James Centre. Five minutes later I get another call to ask where we were. "We're heading for The Bridges, like you said" I told him. "Right, we'll be there in five minutes" he replied. There was about 80 of us and we stopped on the corner and waited. We knew in which direction they'd be coming from. Then almost straight away they appeared in front of us and headed our way. A few of them were carrying clubs and by the looks of it they'd emptied a rubbish skip. There was only about 20 of them and they got slaughtered. The ones that got caught had the shit kicked out of them and a few of our boys had to be pulled off a few of the Hibs boys who were flat out on the pavement. A mate of mine, Big Steve, a West Ham fan that had moved up here years ago, was talking to a couple of Hibs faces the day before the game and he told them that were coming through in a mob and they just laughed and said that they didn't rate us. I bet they did after we hammered them?

A few times they were good and turned up at Ibrox with a solid firm. One game they came marching up Paisley Road West and the police tried to stop them and hold them back, but they just kept on going. They had about 250 top lads and they were dressers as well. I'd say around this time they'd be the best casual mob in Scotland, if not in Britain. They've also had some right battles with Celtic over the years there was a gassing incident at Easter Road and in another attack Celtic casuals gassed a mob of the Hibs C.C.S in Glasgow City centre after Hibs had stopped off after an away game. They chased after the Celtic mob that had launched the gas canister at them but were collared by the old bill before they got their retribution. The whole of the Hibs firm was arrested and taken down to the police station and charged with a `Breach of The Peace` but later these and other charges were dropped.

We've also played them a few times in Cup Finals and they've always been very lively affairs when we've met.

We played them at Hampden and about 70 of us were plotted up in a pub with quite a few of our boys tooled up with coshes and few other bits and pieces. We were waiting for them to pass and we'd had word that they were heading in our direction with a police escort. A couple of police vans came speeding past the pub and we've all charged out onto the street and there was about 60 of them. But the thing we didn't know was there was another 100 of them a couple of hundred yards further up the road. It went mental with it going off all over the place. It was a good one with, I'd say, them just getting the better of it. Thing was they had the numbers that day. It went off right in the middle of the Gorbals, right in the middle of all the flats and estates.

We use to bump into them quite a bit when they passed through Glasgow on their way to an away game. We were playing Arbroath away, which is heading up towards Aberdeen. It was a Cup game and Hibs were playing at Dundee, also in the Cup. About 40 of us stopped in Dundee and got on the phone to the Hibs boys. They were playing Dundee United and were already there in the town. We told them we were in a pub near the train station and their answer to that was "we're here for Dundee, not Rangers". "OK, one of our boys says, how long have Dundee been bigger than Rangers"? A little while later they're back on the phone. By this time a few of our boys had gone off to get the train to our game so there was only about 25 of us left in the pub. Someone shouted that they were heading down the street so I've run out and sure enough, they were coming towards us. The thing was what we all didn't know or care was that the whole thing was being recorded on C.C.T.V. We tore into one another and I'll have to say it was 50-50. It was good. A couple of their boys got taken away in an ambulance but there was no casualties on our side. About 18 of us got arrested for that fight with the police coming to our doors later on. I went to court and got a £1500 fine. A cheap day out?

Hibs' near neighbours, Hearts, are good boys but they just never seem to get it together. A few years back they got off the train in George Square and there was only about 50 of us about and there was about 300 of them. We weren't expecting it, it was probably one of the best results they ever had. Hearts and us have had a few battles a few years back but now we know one another through the Loyalist links. They turn out to oppose the James Connelly Marches so there's a bit of respect between the two of us. You wouldn't really get trouble between the two teams now.

Aberdeen

We've arranged meets with Aberdeen but we've never really met them. They have got some good boys and at home they turn out in big numbers. Their firm, The A.S.C. (The Aberdeen Soccer Casuals) got started around the same time as the Hibs' C.C.S. and some of them claim to be the original casual firm in Scotland. Their main rivals have always been Rangers, Dundee, Hibs and Motherwell.

We took a 60 seater bus up there for a game and we stopped just outside Aberdeen at a place called Stonehaven. We went into a local shop and bought Aberdeen flags and scarves and hung them from the windows of the bus. We got back onto the motorway and saw the police pulling over Rangers' buses and cars to check if they had tickets. We were waved straight through as our Aberdeen flags and scarves hung from the bus. We got into the city centre and we thought we were home and dry but we were spotted by two football intelligence officers as we sat at a set of traffic lights. We were told to pull over and a superintendent came on board and had a look about. He was quite happy to let us go on our way until the two football police pointed out that in fact we weren't Aberdeen fans but the infamous Rangers I.C.F. Casuals. "Really" he replied, still none the wiser. We were taken on the bus to some retail park just outside Aberdeen while the game was going on. Not only that they bought us all a McDonalds meal. They came on board and asked us what we'd like.

Before the game had finished they drove us down near to the ground where the other Rangers buses were parked. At the final whistle hundreds of Rangers fans returned and boarded their buses for home. An Aberdeen mob appeared and came across the grass at the Rangers fans. Our boys on the street have done no more than steam into the Aberdeen mob and scatter them everywhere. We've all sat on the bus watching in disbelief.

Aberdeen have been down to Glasgow a few times but will only turn up if they've got big numbers. Aberdeen has a strong connection with Spurs so quite a few of them go down to London for a weekend and shop for all the latest gear. I don't know how this close link with Spurs started, but I have heard it said that it was something to do with the transfer of Steve Archibald from Aberdeen to Tottenham, many years ago.

They once took 70 boys down to London for a Spurs v West Ham game. Tottenham have also been up here with Aberdeen. We came across a few of Aberdeen's boys at a game when we took 70 boys up there on a train and most of the Aberdeen mob seem to have cockney accents. Me and me mate went up there another time for a game but the match had already kicked off by the time we arrived. As soon as we stepped off the train the police nabbed us. The police knew who we were and arrested us on suspicion of a breach of the peace. That was well worth the three-hour train journey. They held us until midnight then let us go with out charge. None of the Aberdeen lads were arrested who were hanging around outside the station when we arrived. After the game, I'm told it went toe to toe before the Old Bill came and broke it up. We've had a few big rows with Aberdeen and as I said, we've arranged a few meets with them but for one reason or another we've never had a pre-arranged meet with them. Usually we'll arrange somewhere and they'll go another way. The clashes we have had with them have just been by pure chance. They used to be good but they're shit now and they've fell away with no real mob to talk of.

Motherwell

Years ago Motherwell were good. It's only about half an hour outside Glasgow and they were well naughty. We took a good mob over there for a game and before the game nothing really happened so the bulk of us went back on the train. About 30 of us found a boozer and were just sitting in there having a drink. Next minute one of our boys is outside getting leathered by a mob of Motherwell. I've run out and gone into them and one of our lot was waving a metal crutch about and one of their lads ended up with 69 stitches in his neck and down his back. That was quite a nasty one.

They used to turn up at Ibrox and were as game as fuck. Their mob was a mainly Protestant mob called `The SS` which stood for `The Saturday Service. ` At one time their boys had their own flute band which was made up with purely boys from the S.S. They were supposedly very right wing in their views and it was said that they had links with the B.N.P. and Combat 18. Years ago we'd go to places like Motherwell and just swamp the place. Now it's all seated and it's harder for us to get in, what with away fans limited ticket allocations and that. They used to have a connection with Leeds for some reason but don't ask me why.

A few of their boys in May 86 got badly cut by some of our lot. They came one season to us in a mob, about 500 strong, and we've met them at the back of the away end and it's just gone absolutely mental. They had a huge big lump of a man at the front who was pushing people out of the way. One of ours stepped forward and give it to him with a blade. Suddenly he knew he'd been cut and panicked and blood bubbles are coming out of his mouth. He was shitting himself. A lot of the teams like Motherwell and Aberdeen and Dundee didn't like coming to Glasgow to play us or Celtic because they knew the chances were that they could get slashed or cut if they got caught.

Falkirk

Falkirk's only about 35 minutes on a train outside Glasgow and their mob's The Falkirk Fear. Fear my arse! They probably fear themselves. They couldn't sort out their sock draw or fight sleep. As a town for a night out it ain't too bad and I know a few of the boys over there and they're O.K. They're another Protestant firm. They could, on a good day, put 40 or 50 good lads together. They're, say, on a par with Airdrie or Dundee.

St. Mirren

St. Mirren, years ago, had a great mob. We'd go through there and we'd take hundreds and they'd turn out 300 or more and there'd be running battles in the streets. We'd eventually turn them over just by sheer weight of numbers but they were well up for it. Their mob just weren't football fans and it would be the locals as well turning out for us lot.

Morton

Morton are another Loyalist mob who have a nice tight little firm. They took over 100 in a firm to Airdrie and tried to take Airdrie's home terrace. One of their main boys, Cass, used to come to a few Rangers games and a few of their lads join up with us on the marches and parades.

Kilmarnock

Killie have also had a decent casual mob and when they first got promoted they put up a good show against our lot. Me and me mate never went as we were going on holiday abroad and we had to go and pick up our flight tickets. I told the rest of the lads to watch themselves as the cunts have got a good firm. It turns out we went there with 40 lads and Kilmarnock turned out over 100 strong and our lot got turned over by them. We played them at Hampden and their lads came on a couple of double Decker buses and done well. We also went to Killie a few years after we came unstuck and this time we were all together and had a right tight firm. We came out the station and they were waiting but this time we smashed them all up the road and a couple of flares and thunder flashes and a few squirts of the gear sent them packing.

Dundee

We've had a couple of things with them. We played them in the Cup once and they got on the phone and told us to meet them at Bairds, which is a Celtic pub. A few of the lads went over there and there was a bit of a scuffle and Dundee did well. I did hear that they'd come on a double Decker bus but it was only half full and that the Old Bill rounded them up and nicked the lot of them after they found all sorts of weapons on board. We waited up near Ibrox for them but they never showed. I don't blame them. We caught a few of them in another encounter and two of their lads got pretty badly slashed. I'd put them on a par with Airdrie.

Partick Thistle

Partick is in the East end of Glasgow and we've had a couple of good ones with them. They set about some of our boys on the subway and we were all in a pub in the town and the boys came in and told us of what had gone on. We jumped on the subway and found the pub they were in and they came out carrying baseball bats. They normally fight with the smaller teams like Airdrie, Allola and the likes of Clyde.

Most teams that come to Ibrox are only too happy to get a police escort and once they're safely in the ground they sing their hearts out. Aberdeen on the other hand take it that bit further and sing songs about the Ibrox disaster, which is pretty bad. Not every team that comes sell out their allocation of tickets for the away end. We got our own back on Aberdeen when we won the Title there, which was the first one in our 9 in a row. Terry Butcher and Brian Laudrup were in that side. We went up to Aberdeen the night before. We were up on the main street and they came piling towards us and Rangers run them all up Union Street. A few distress flares fired at them helped them on their way. The same a couple of seasons back when Aberdeen came on the pitch up there and one or two of them lent over the fencing and punched an old boy from Rangers and broke his glasses. That to me just shows how brave they are.

BOBBY

I was the first Hearts Casual in 1984. It was the year the Casual Soccer Firm (C.S.F.) started. We'd never really had an organized mob before that. There'd been a few Skinheads running around years before calling themselves the Hearts Service Crew.

When I was a young kid Hearts were the top firm up here above Rangers, Celtic and Hibs. We were the tops. In the 70s no-one could touch us.

The first game I ever went to was when I was about 7 and Hearts lost 5-1 in a European tie. All my family were Rangers fans. I'm from one of the biggest Protestant families in Edinburgh and I'm the only that that follows Hearts. The big rivalry in Edinburgh is obviously us and Hibs. In the 70s we ran the show and in the 80s and 90s it changed to Hibs, and now it's 50-50. It went quiet for years but now the youth in the city have kicked it off again.

The best row I've ever seen at football was when 50 of us from the Scottish National Firm when down to a Man City v Middlesborough game. It was an F.A. Cup game and it went off for 15 minutes.

We found a boozer and spoke to one of Boro's main boys on the phone. We didn't leave the boozer and after the game a mob of Man City and Boro came down the main road towards us singing "England." We came out chanting "Scotland" and it just went off. In the end the Old Bill had to escort us out of Manchester. That day was just fucking mental.

Another time we were in Blackpool and we had it with 50 Portsmouth lads. We found them in a pub and one of our lads fired a flare gun into the pub to get them out. It just went. After that the police escorted us all the way back to Glasgow.

The best mob I've ever seen in Edinburgh was Rangers at Hibs for the last game of the season. Rangers came through with a 150 strong mob and got right outside the Hibs boys main boozer but they wouldn't come out. They didn't want to play. The Old Bill didn't even know we were there. I found the boys a little club which I know, and afterwards the owner says to me "Bobby you've just bought in the worst 150 football hooligans in the country but they're perfect gentlemen and they're welcome back anytime."

I'm 38 years old now and I've always hated Celtic. It's about what they stand for. When they come through to Edinburgh they have to have police protection. We hate them here. We have no respect for them, none whatsoever.

Football hooliganism is still alive up here. We played Motherwell at home and we ended up drinking in the West End. A Hibs mob of about 30 turned up and it just went. It was even numbers. It was their main boys and our main faces and it went right off.

I think the Banning Orders and C.C.T.V. have fucked it now. I've just finished a 4 year Banning Order and now I'm back.

CHAPTER 6
THE SCOTTISH NATIONAL FIRM

A lot of the Rangers' boys never really went to the Scotland international games simply because us lot are more into flying the Union Jack and wearing the England football jersey. Wear an England shirt in a pub or club where there's Celtic or Hibs fans and watch them cunts get the hump. It works a treat. I've done it myself on more than one occasion. They fucking hate it. A lot of the wee teams used to make up the Scottish firm, teams like Falkirk, Airdrie, Dundee and Hibs and Aberdeen.

We played Sweden in Gothenburg and we smashed the Swede's Black Army. But I was never one for going to International games.

When I was a boy my dad took me to Scotland v Northern Ireland and the whole end we were stood on sang The Sash. I think the small teams that made up the national firm only went because their own sides were never very successful and watching Scotland they maybe thought that would give them something to cheer about. Well, that's chooktas for ya.

When we were waiting at the airport to come back from Sweden, one of the Rangers lads was walking past a group of Hibs and they started singing Baldie Casual Bastards. He, in reply, sang Rule Britannia and that was it. The whole lot went up and there was a massive punch up. We fucking smashed them. They didn't know how many of us lot was there. We'd been drinking around the corner out of sight. There was two plane loads of fans fighting in the departure lounge. In the end near on everyone was deported and had to make their way home by ferry. Me and a Hearts boy managed to get on the flight home.

I've been down to London for a Scotland game at Wembley. Us and Hearts got down there early and were the first ones in Trafalgar Square. We all drove down in cars and met up. A lot of us didn't go to the game, we just stayed around the square drinking. It was kicking off with all sorts of English mobs. At one time a mob of Chelsea were across the other side of the road and I knew a few of them so I gave them a wave and went the other way. There was quite a few main faces in their firm who are as game as fuck. The thing was we had a good mob but all the teams there seemed to all stick with their own lads.

There was a mob of Aberdeen there who had a few Tottenham lads with them and they'd heard Rangers were about. "Let's do them" one of them said to us, not knowing we were Rangers. We says to them "well, we're Rangers so let's just us and you have it and leave everyone else out, but they wouldn't have it.

Leicester had a good fair sized firm there and we done them. We had a bit of a dash with Man Utd and done them. It was a good day out with plenty of action.

We played Wales at Kilmarnock and one of the boys got one of Cardiff's main lads' mobile number. It was only a friendly so the Scottish F.A. wasn't expecting a big crowd so the choice of venue was Killies' ground. We phoned this Taffy up and he informed us that Cardiff's Soul Crew wouldn't be coming up but he'd heard that Swansea's mob were making the trip north. They did turn up but Dundee's mob got to them first and smashed them everywhere. We never see them. We had a good mob out that day and met up in Glasgow and then went over on the train. When we got there we found a pub and a few Kilmarnock lads turned up and asked if it was all right if they came with us.

When we played England up here our mob met up about 10 in the morning. We went over to the main station and there was groups of boys everywhere. A mob came in off the train and they were asked who they were. "Cardiff" one of them said, and walked away. They then came out with different teams' names and kidded on they weren't looking for trouble. We followed them and as we turned a corner they turned around and began bouncing up and down in the middle of the road. "Come on then they" shouted, "we're England". That was it. We went for them and they scattered. Three or four of them got caught and took a battering. We ran 150 of them without a punch being thrown. We did hear that the bulk of this English firm were from Derby County. Later on Chelsea and West Ham had a bit of a do. I'm not sure if it was the same game at Hampden but a mob of English got into the enclosure where a lot of Scottish fans were and it went off for a long time before the Old Bill moved in.

Around 11.30 at night about 20 of us were having a walk about. The bulk of the lads were Celtic but a few were mates of mine and the rest hated me because of my Rangers connections. I think they'd of rather had a row with me than with the English. Someone had seen a bus parked down by the station with a group of lads hanging around, waiting to get on it. As we walked past it words were exchanged and then a few punches were thrown. One of the English went down clutching his face with blood oozing through his fingers. He was screaming in pain. One of ours had swung a chain around and it had caught this bloke in the eye. The police turned up and we were well away up the road when they pulled us over. We denied being involved in any trouble so they took all our names and addresses and sent us on our way. Later the next night I had some trouble in a night club and the police were called. One of the police on duty that night recognized me from the incident with the English the day before and my appearance seem to interest him, and plus what I had on matched the description of the bloke that had been swinging the chain around. I was arrested and taken to court on the Monday morning and I was remanded for 7 days. It's what's known in Scotland as a "7 day lie down". I then got a knock back in court and was held for 3 months on remand in Barlinie jail, which is probably the toughest jail in Scotland, if not in Britain. The place is infamous. There was also maybe 20 English fans remanded in there after the game. They were also being held on the 3 months remand rule, which is a law we have in Scotland.

One of the English arrested was a big black bloke who'd been shown on the T.V. news, being held down by 7 coppers. He'd been doing a lot of fighting that day, and he put up quite a struggle. It's a rough, tough jail and you don't get many black geezers in there. When you first get booked in, the screws take you up to a cell which is used as a store room where there's blankets and pillows. The black man was pushed inside and the door shut and waiting inside were a few cons who proceeded to kick the shit out of him. I've never heard screams like it. They give him a right going over.

The rest of the English didn't eat for the first 3 days because all sorts of shit was put in their food, spit, glass, cigarette butts, piss. You name it, it was put in their grub. Then the rest of the cons said enough was enough and everyone was all right. It was pointed out to a few idiots that they were locked up the same as us and were no different.

The screws could be right cunts in there and I saw them drag a con off to The Wendy House, which was basically a cell made of toughened plastic which you could see into. It was for prisoners on suicide watch. The screws dragged this boy along the landing and bent his arm so far up his back that they snapped it. Prisoners on remand would be given blue shirts to wear and convicted prisoners got red and white striped shirts that, from a distance, looked pink. It was two to a cell and then after a while I was moved to a single cell. I soon found a boy I knew from football so I had a familiar face around me which made it a bit easier.

I was in with Carlisle's top boy, Rouledge, who was known as The Fatman. He was a good laugh and had been banged up for all sorts of things. A few years later we took a coach down to a Carlisle v Falkirk pre-season friendly the coach was made up of Rangers, Hibs and about 10 Falkirk lads. Carlisle is only about a 2-hour drive from Glasgow, so we drove down on the morning of the game. As soon as we got there the old bill had us wrapped up. They put us in an escort and walked us of towards the ground as we walked past a pub a couple of the lads nipped in to use the toilet, next minute they've come flying out of the door a few of the Carlisle boys came out behind them and that prick Dodd was with them, some ones launched a bottle and hit him straight in the face it was a great shot. We backed them off into the pub and the police came in and opened up with gas, and my big mate Trotter caught it straight in the face. They came out of the pub as we were being taken up the ground but they didn't' let us in they just bought the bus up loaded us up and fucked us of out of it. A few of the Carlisle lads arranged to meet us later just over the border, but they failed to turn up. The next time we bumped into Doddies boys was in Trafalgar Square when England played Scotland, I rate Carlisle, for a small team they've' got a good little outfit. I met Dodds brother in their pub `The Beehive` I think its called. I was on holiday near Carlisle and popped in there for a drink and got chatting to a few of the boys as you do and one of them was his brother. His brothers older then him with a tidier hairdo and a bit more sensible I did hear later that a few of their older lads weren't too happy about me being in their pub.

The boredom inside was horrible and the prison stank and was a crumbling shit hole. You were banged up some day's 24 hours and you were lucky to get exercise once a week. You'd slop out in the morning, have your meals, normally in your cell, and sit and watch the rain piss in through the metal bars on the narrow window the rain would flood ya cell and soak ya bed and blankets.

I was first banged up with a junkie who used to grind his teeth in his sleep. I'm only a light sleeper so all night I couldn't sleep listening to this cunt. The next day I told the screw who opened up to move this cunt otherwise he would have a murder on his hands. He was moved.

I got to know a few serious faces in there. A lot of the boys were in for armed robbery and all sorts but they were a good bunch of lads. The one bit of trouble I had was when I was working on the hot plate dishing up the food and this boy took two dinners. We had a bit of an argument but the screws quickly broke it up. A few of the boys hinted that I couldn't let this boy get away with taking the piss so the next morning when he was in the shower I battered him with a heavy duty battery in a sock. That sorted him out and taught him not to take the piss. The boy never ever looked at me after that and kept right out of my way.
I done 4 months on remand before going back to court where the

police could offer no evidence, so it was basically thrown out of court.

About 60 of us went out to the World Cup out in France where Scotland were playing in Bordeaux. We based ourselves in Spain and for this game we went by coach from Salou. All was going well till we reached the Spanish/French border and one of the boys noticed a police helicopter following us overhead. Then a police escort took us all the way into Bordeaux and held us in the car park of a police station, then moved us to a warehouse. They bought us in a meal and a few of the boys started to get a bit restless and demanded to know what was going on. We'd caused no trouble so there was no need for all this bollocks. They bought in all these Robocops with their body armour and batons and gas. We explained we were in France for the Scotland game so they bought in a big telly so we could watch the game. Talk about things getting lost in translation.

After the game we were loaded back onto the coach and were escorted back to the Spanish border. It kicked off when we were in Spain one night with a few of the locals and one of our boys was knocked down by a couple of Spanish lads in a car. Our lot, were fighting with some bouncers outside a nightclub and the locals joined in, as they do. We heard Stokes' firm were stopping in Barcelona and a few of the boys were organizing a little something with them, but it never happened. Our little outing on the bus even made the Scottish tabloids with pictures of us splashed across the front pages with all sorts of headlines calling us all sorts of things. Did we care? Did we fuck? My name was prominent in these reports. Reporters were waiting for the boys at the airport on their return from Spain and one of the headlines read "David Carrick and the Dirty Dozen Still Hell Bent on Trouble". Thing was I'd left Spain early because of work commitments so I wasn't even on the plane with the rest of the boys.

It wasn't Hadrian's Wall, which kept us out of England when we played in the end it was the English F.A. I think it was a sad day for every Scottish football fan when the Home Internationals were bought to an end. We've played a lot of top European teams up here in Scotland but not many have bought a firm. We saw the Germans boasting on T.V. that they were coming to Glasgow for trouble and they did turn up, but you couldn't get near them What we did see of them was their dress sense was unbelievable. They had these mullet hair cuts and orange track suits and black and white shell suits. They looked a right bunch of pricks. There was the odd scuffle here and there outside a few bars but it was quickly broken up by the police.

In the 1990s Rangers, Hearts and a few of the smaller teams came together as the S.N.F. (Scottish National Firm) and even a few of the Hibernian boys joined the alliance and the collaboration made the Scottish firm a major player on the international stage. But it was short lived and died a death through in fighting and one thing and another. Nowadays the Tartan Army is still on the march but it's mainly the supporters of the smaller clubs that follow Scotland and its all ginger beards and kilts.

PEDRO

I was adopted and came to Glasgow from London in the 60s. I used to hang around the town with a group of boys who were mixed, some Rangers and some Celtic. There was about 40 or 50 of us North side boys who were as game as fuck. That's when I first met Davie.

Hibs were the kiddies in the 80s but the I.C.F. at Rangers took over. We had a right battle with them in the League Cup Semi Final and I had part of my ear cut off so I'll never forget that game. Without a doubt we had the strongest and the best firm. In the last 5 or 6 years nobody has matched us.

Don't worry about Aberdeen who claim they were the tops. They've never run fuck all. From the early 90s we run the show up here. When we played Aberdeen at Ibrox we pulled a mob together of well over a thousand and out of that we had 350 to 400 good boys and the rest were hangers on.

People rave about Celtic's numbers but they're shit. They're not an organized mob, they're an unorganized gang. The top boys in Celtic know who we are and have no answer to us. They know when we play them that we're coming. As a mob I wouldn't piss on them.

Hibs' mob has gone into decline. We played them once, on the last day of the season at their place, and we attacked the pub where they were drinking and they pulled the curtains and wouldn't come out. That would never have happened a few years ago. They used to be as game as fuck.

Aberdeen still try to turn out at home for us but away they don't do it any more.

The football hooligan scene in Scotland is more or less finished now but we do have a very, very very good youth division at Rangers who do their own thing. There are good young boys coming through now.

With Internationals I'm not interested in the Scotland team, that's for the sheep across in Edinburgh. Most Rangers' fans are not interested in Scotland games and singing "here we go" and "Doe a deer" and all that shit. What the fuck is that all about? Doe a fucking deer and wearing a kilt? That's not what following a football team is all about.

BIG GEOFF

Chelsea played Rangers in 1985 at Stamford Bridge in a fund raising game for the Bradford fire disaster. I went along to the game and met up with a lot of the Rangers boys. I never knew any of them before the game and to tell you the truth wasn't expecting any trouble between the two sides. There's always been this link with Rangers and Chelsea and around this time Chelsea had quite a large National Front following and also followed the Loyalist links closely. Rangers too had a big pro British following. The two sets of fans seem to share the same political beliefs, plus Chelsea's tradition of signing Scottish players helped forge a mutual admiration between the fans. The other thing we had in common was the dislike of the I.R.A. In the end it was a brilliant night down at Stamford Bridge. A lot of friendships were formed that night.

Whilst serving in the British Army I met up with a guy that lived in South Belfast and he got me interested in the Orange Order. Basically it all stemmed from there. I used to go over to Belfast on the 12th of July and do all the marches and stay with my friend. I also got to find out about the association between local side, Linfield and Glasgow Rangers. If Rangers go to Northern Ireland to play a friendly they will play Linfield. I then joined the Rangers' supporters Club in London, which gave me cheap travel and the chance of match tickets.

There's Rangers' Supporters Clubs all over the country but the London one is huge. Arsenal fans, Spurs fans, Millwall fans who join forget their differences with one another and come together to support Rangers. It's a well-organized club with lots of Scottish fans living in and working in London joining up and there's also quite a few members from Northern Ireland as well.

The first game I went to up there was an old firm game at Parkhead. A few of the Rangers lads even went as far as giving their own tickets up for the game to some of the Chelsea lads that had gone up for the game but didn't have tickets, and there's a few Chelsea season ticket holders that do the same with Rangers fans when they come down for a game at the Bridge. The game against Celtic was unbelievable. There was such a buzz around the ground. There was no trouble before the game but afterwards it was kicking off. Rangers won the match so the pissed off Celtic fans had the right hump but the Old Bill have it pretty much sussed out.

We drank in a few bars over near Ibrox before the game and was made more than welcome. We drank in 'The District bar', 'The Louden Arms', 'The Grapes' and then got onto the Metro to Parkhead.

Afterwards the celebrations were wild and people were going mental, people down south talk about the rivalries between Man City and Man Utd and Spurs and Arsenal and West Ham and Millwall, but this was something else. It moved up another level and you could almost taste the hatred. It was in a different league in terms of atmosphere. The songs aimed at one another are pure hatred. They were singing anti-British songs and 'The Soldier' song and we sang 'King Billy's on the Wall' and anti Pope songs and 'The Sash'.

The place to be when Celtic play at Ibrox is in the lower enclosure because you're right next to them. I'd put that game at Ibrox as one of the best atmospheres I'd ever experienced at a football match. It makes the hair on the back of your neck stand up on end. I've been to Aberdeen with Rangers where the atmosphere isn't quite as intimidating as Celtic, but it is quite threatening. Aberdeen and Rangers just don't get on. It's been well publicized about Chelsea fans being involved in clashes with Aberdeen fans up there. Some Chelsea fans have even been pulled over by the police on their way by coaches up to Aberdeen and have been searched and turned back on the motorway.

I still have my own political views on Ulster and I favour the U.V.F. (The Ulster Volunteer Force) purely because of its history. It was formed after the Ulster Covenant was signed by Sir Edward Carson in 1912. It was basically to stop home rule in Ireland. At one time the whole of Ireland was governed by Westminster but the British government was going to allow the whole of Ireland, including Ulster, home rule, but over half a million people signed a petition to protest against this happening. The Protestant population in Ulster didn't want this and wanted to be governed by Westminster. They didn't want anything to do with being ruled by a political party in Dublin, but the British government were adamant that this would go ahead, even though many people in the province were dead against it. Even British politicians were sympathetic to the Protestant cause in Ulster, but it still went ahead.

In 1914 twenty five thousand rifles and 3 million rounds of ammunition was smuggled into Ulster through various ports from Germany. This was for the set up of the original Ulster Volunteer Force. They were prepared to take on any one that was trying to impose home rule, but the First World War came along and for the time being Ulster men and the U.V.Fs attention was turned to fighting the Germans. They joined the rest of Britain in its battle against Germany. Lots of young guys from Ulster who were too young to join the British Army, set up the Y.C.V. (The Young Citizen Volunteers) and were the junior branch of the U.V.F. They lied about their age just to go off and see some action. They were quite prepared to die for their country. They classed themselves as British and still do. It's the same as a Catholic in Northern Ireland. He will tell you he is Irish so what's the problem with a Protestant from Northern

Ireland classing themselves as British? It's exactly the same as a Scotsman or a Welshman classing themselves as British. If you go to South Belfast and Sandy Row you'll see the kerb stones painted red, white and blue. That's how patriotic the people are out there. The British government declared the U.V.F. a terrorist organization, I believe in the late 60s.

July 1916 saw the start of the Battle of the Somme. The only unit to take German territory that day was the 36th Ulster Division who were basically made up of the Ulster Volunteer Force, along with the Royal Elinskine Fusiliers, The Royal Irish Rifles and the Mid-Antrim volunteers who were also made up of the U.V.F. These boys fought for and alongside the rest of the British army and between the 1st of July and October of 1916 these boys won 9 Victoria Crosses, but to this day they are seen as a terrorist organization. To me that is absolutely scandalous. You cannot re-write history and these boys are a part of our history whether you like it or not. There were many people who fought for Britain in both World Wars and that includes not just Ulster men but Irish people from the Republic of Ireland. These people won Victoria Crosses and yet their history has been wiped out. To Loyalist people like me what they did will never ever be forgotten. Their memories live on in our memories. You cannot wipe that out. The U.V.F. didn't want home rule all those years ago and were prepared to fight for their cause and stay British.

Nowadays you have the U.D.A. (The Ulster Defence Association) who in the beginning were similar to the U.V.F. Now there's off shoots like Ulster Freedom Fighters, who weren't prepared to talk. They wanted action. There's also the Ulster Volunteer Force splinter groups like the Loyalist Volunteer Force and The Red Hand Commandos who were all fed up with what was going on and wanted action. But within the said groups there's always been trouble with disagreements and disputes and in –fighting leading to violence amongst one another. A lot of people from Ulster show their support and their Britishness by going over to Scotland and following Glasgow Rangers. Lots of them are now coming over to London and are following Chelsea and a few of the Chelsea lads go over to Ulster for the marching season and are made very welcome. Some are just Orangemen and belong to the Orange Order and have no political affiliation. It's just like being in the Freemasons. You can go anywhere in the World as an Orangeman and go into an Orange Lodge. Politics does not stand between the Orange Order. A U.V.F man and a U.D.A. man could drink together or side by side in an Orange Lodge and their own political views would be left at the front door.

To this day I'm still friends with lots of the Rangers lads and class them as some of my close pals. My dad got me started in all this because when he done his National Service he served with The Royal Ulster Rifles who were at one time The Royal Irish Rifles who won all those V.C.s My dad spoke a lot about his time in Northern Ireland and he loved the place. I wish I could get out there a bit more nowadays and my political beliefs will never change they've still the same.

The lads on their way to Germany for the Borussia Mönchengladbach game,

Me and my boy, Jamie with Ally McCoist.

In Salou for the Word Cup in France. Mostly Rangers, Hibs and Hearts.

Borussia Mönchengladbach – Mark, Geemac and Allan

A few of the boys out for England's third World Cup game 2006.

Me and Sandy, a real good mate.

Me and Colin Bell.

Bobby Thomson (far left) Martin King and Chris from Hearts next to me.

It's good to be back – I thought I was on a ban.

I don't know who the wee geezer in the middle is but he kindly gave Martin King a ticket for the game.

Martin King buys Celtic and hands it over to me to run as Rangers Feeder club.

Knock it down and build a car-park or super-market.

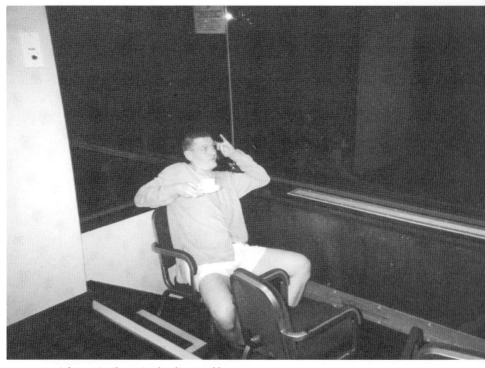

A night out in Ibrox, in the directors' box.

Some of the boys in Ibrox directors' box – Christmas night out.

Amsterdam v Ajax – a flute band marched around the Red Light District.

Amsterdam – met up with a few Chelsea boys – Stewart Glass with the shades on.

Amsterdam – Colin (who's dead now), Smoothie and me. Broony got the jail so we put his clothes on, took photo and put them back.

Me, Warren, Flynie, Smoothie and Broony.

A flute band in Amsterdam.

A fund raiser at the Bristol pub in Glasgow for the prisoners' wives.

"ULTRAS ON THE FERRY" Me and Smoothie going to Brugge.

I.C.F. night out. Most of us were banned for life, but we took the piss by hiring out a suite at Ibrox – Me and Warren enjoy a drink.

CHAPTER 7

RANGERS IN EUROPE

I've followed Rangers in Europe and had some right laughs and rows along the way. We were playing Brugge out in Belgium so about 60 of us caught the train down to Dover and on the way it kicked off with some boys from Blackpool who were on their way out to the game to follow Rangers. Fuck knows what started it but it kicked off and these Blackpool lads took a bit of a kicking. A few of the lads said that they had picked on a few Rangers fans who were sitting away from us lot and that the Blackpool lads were trying to take a few liberties.

Anyway, we caught the boat and then the train through to Brugge. We got off and we've walked through the city centre and headed towards the ground. It was a good 40 minute walk, which none of us realized was so far. The way we've walked us bought us out at the home end of their stadium. We had no Old Bill with us and the Belgians hadn't sussed us. On a corner was a pub and outside was a group of blokes standing around drinking and looking like they were up for a row. They've seen us heading towards them "Come on Rangers" a couple of them shouted, so we've charged at the pub and they've all bolted inside, but what they've done is gone in one door and come back out again through a side door. Then it's gone fucking mental and toe to toe. It was all fists and no weapons. I think I only saw one bottle thrown. The Old Bill arrived and surrounded the pub and pushed us up the road. One of ours threw a bottle at them, which landed above the door and they chanted "Celtic, Celtic Celtic".

After the game they came around to our end of the ground and we're mobbed up and stood on a bit of waste ground about 300 handed. But our shirts and scarves and normal fans, and beer monsters have come out before us and all we've seen is the Belgians being run everywhere by our Barmies. We all got split up as the Belgian police came in all heavy handed. Four of us found ourselves walking around the back streets and alleyways. There was one narrow, dark side street with trees and bushes overhanging we passed along. At the top of the street we could make out about 300 shadowy figures moving about in the dark as if they were planning an ambush. We doubled back before we were spotted and jumped on a Rangers' supporters' bus, parked up on the side of the street. It was well dodgy.

I went back out there a few seasons later with Chelsea and we met up with a few of the boys who were cut and bruised and said they'd had a bit of a row with some Belgians who were tooled up with hammers and blades. So looking back we didn't do to bad out there with Rangers?

Another one was when we played Ajax in Amsterdam. That was right nasty. We had about 100 boys the night before the game and we had it with about 50 Ajax. They had a mixed mob of young and old and they had quite a few black faces with them. We were drinking in

Hooters bar and they came to the door and we piled out and chased them over the bridge and into the Red Light district. The next day it was well naughty and one of our boys got stabbed in the leg when we were fighting with them.

The day of the game Ajax came looking for us. Even the Dutch Old Bill told us to watch ourselves as the Ajax boys were a bit handy with the blades. They came at us from every direction after we left a bar and headed for the ground. They were trying to get at us through little lanes and the riot police were heading them off. There was about 80 of us on the Metro and the police told us to get off at the stop before the stadium because getting off at the ground was too dodgy. But we didn't take a blind bit of notice and stayed on. We came out in a nice tight group and straight away fronted a few of their boys. "Where's ya firm"? we asked, and they ran off. Next thing we see their massive mob coming towards us. It was like the start of the London Marathon heading in our direction. We stood for as long as we could and as our numbers dwindled to about 25 we just got swamped and had to leg it. They chased us all the way to the Rangers' end of the ground. There were some big gates and we dived behind them and they were slammed shut. Next thing the riot police came running down the road with this massive Ajax firm chasing them. As they passed us we came out through the gates and steamed into the tail end of them. The Old Bill returned and separated the two mobs. Fucking hell, it was like something out of Laurel and Hardy or the Keystone Cops. It would have been laughable if I hadn't of been there.

After the game it was kicking off all night around the Red Light area. The Dutch just wouldn't leave off. We had our work cut out to mind our backs. There was about 60 of us that stuck together. We'd run one mob of them and 5 minutes later another mob of them would appear from somewhere else. The local police were all right before the game and a few of the lads had photos done with the them. We even had the Dutch riot police posing for photos wearing Rangers' scarves. They were as good as gold until a couple of our football intelligence officers turned up and started trying to give orders and throw their weight about. They were telling their Dutch counterparts to film me and a couple of others and the Dutch were asking why as we hadn't done anything. Our Old Bill were acting like right arseholes and made right cunts of themselves. They grabbed hold of one of our boys and started getting a bit heavy but the Dutch riot police stepped in and told our football Old Bill to let him go. A full can of beer was thrown at the coppers as they sulked off and it hit one of them straight on the back of the head. "Fucking arsehole," he shouted. As he turned around. "Who's done it, who's done it"? he yelled. We were pissing ourselves laughing.

We stopped in Amsterdam for the night and we got talking to a few of the Ajax boys who had a few beers with us and told us they well rated Rangers after our visit to Holland.

We have also played P.S.V. Eindhoven in Holland and went over by train. On the night of the game about 50 of us got off at the main station and walked through the streets. In no time at all their mob was in front of us. "Come on" someone shouted on our side, and launched a full can of beer into them. We charged into them and the rest of their mob came into us from the side. I got grabbed and nicked almost straight away and I was carted off to jail. The rest of the boys carried on fighting their way down towards the ground. I'd been seen throwing the can of beer into them so I couldn't really complain but as I was being released from the police station the Dutch Old Bill were bringing 22 of our lot in. I was walking out reading my charge sheet, or trying to read it because it was in double Dutch, when I was spotted by one of our football coppers. "Where's he going"? the copper asked his Dutch colleague. "He's been charged and now he's free to go" he replied. The football copper grabbed me and pushed me back into the lift inside the station. "You fucking bastard" he screamed into my face. See this cunt, he desperately wanted everyone jailed. The Dutch thankfully didn't listen to him and let me go but this cunt had steam coming out of his ears. There was nothing he could do, much to his disappointment.

Some of the cells in the nick had tellys in them and they were letting those banged up watch the game. Mine never had a telly so they bought in a radio so that I could listen to the game. That was until Rangers scored and the copper came in and switched it off. It seemed even the police out there were big football fans and were so different to our Old Bill who could learn a thing or two from them.

I never went back for my court appearance and not long afterwards I received a letter informing me I was now on the Netherlands wanted list. Maybe Dog the Bounty hunter will come looking for me?

When we played Feyenoord in a European game I got hold of one of their lads' mobile numbers. They turned up in Glasgow for the first game about 80 handed and they even had a few Aberdeen with them. It kicked off inside the ground and normal supporters were steaming into them. It was live on the T.V. and we stayed out of the way and watched it in the pub. After the game one of our lads followed a mob of them to a pub, which was right out of the way. We got a call telling us where they were so about 70 of us set off to find them. We had no Old Bill with us and by the reports we'd got they had no Old Bill with them. We were told there was about 80 or 90 of them with about 15 Aberdeen with them. As we walked towards the pub they must have seen us coming and they've emptied out of the pub and by the looks of it they had some right big lumps in their mob. At the front they had a big black Maori type who was about 6ft 8" tall. I heard one of his mates shout "Jerrel". Me and me mate Warren and

Sandy were at the front. I looked at him. "This will be good" I said, and with that we charged. Without a punch being thrown they ran and their mob split into two. The big black geezer disappeared into thin air like the rest of their mob but a few Aberdeen got caught and took a slap. We had the right hump with them no good dogs.

In the return leg we didn't take many out there but by all accounts our boys done well and went into one of Feyenoord's main bars and smashed it up. Our lads said the Dutch had a bigger mob out for Rangers than they did when they played Chelsea. I think they got the right hump for what happened to them in Glasgow. Our boys were on the station after the game and apparently there were 300 Feyenoord trying to get into them at one end of the station and another 300 trying to get in through the other side and it was only the Dutch riot Old Bill who were holding them back, otherwise there would have been murders.

Marseille were another team to turn up at Ibrox and most of their firm had on baseball jackets with a clenched fist design on the back with a lightning bolt going through it. They looked like something out of Grease or Happy Days. The Fonz and his pals from the diner had come to town! They had about 150 in George Square late at night and no-one knew anything about it. None of us even knew they were here. This was after the game and no one was really expecting them. For the away leg a few of the boys went out there and although there was a bit of missile throwing from the French inside the ground, nothing really went on outside. It was mostly the young local Arabs looking for trouble. They'd bounce about in the road in front of you and chuck stuff, but when it came to a toe to toe they didn't want to know.

I remember the two Leeds Utd fans who were stabbed and died out in Istanbul just a few hours before their team were due to play

Galatasavay in the semi finals of the UEFA Cup. How the fuck that game was allowed to continue after that audacity I'll never know.

We played Fenerbace the year after and again, hundreds of young Turks turned out for the Rangers fans. That made the trip.

At Ibrox the police surrounded us in a pub we were all drinking in and kept us in and wouldn't allow us to move, but the local Turks were out in Glasgow wearing their shirts and chanting and singing. Going to watch football in Turkey or Greece wouldn't appeal to me. I wouldn't fancy it, it's not football as far as I'm concerned. I've always fancied seeing us play in The Nou Camp at Barcelona or The Camp Nou as it's now known, or out in Madrid. That would be something special but we never seem to progress past the first stages of the Champions League. We always seem to go out to some unknown Norwegian minnows or some team from Aberbiezian or somewhere.

We played Munchenglabach from Germany a few years back and there was a few scuffles but nothing much. We played Borrusia Dortmund and they were the same. They've got a bit of a friendship thing with Celtic for some reason. A couple of the Germans had Celtic tops on and we didn't take too kindly to that and they got punched about a bit. None of the Italians have been up here. Perhaps their Ultras don't travel?

We went to Paris the night before we played P.S.G. and stayed in a hotel just off the city centre. There was a French baggage handlers' strike so we had to fly to Dublin, spend the night there and the next day fly to Brussels, and then from there we took the train to Paris. That was fun and games. We got to Dublin about 10 at night and we explained to the people running the hotel that we were Rangers' fans on our way to France to watch a game so could they tell us a pub where it wasn't full of Celtic memorabilia and the like. So they sent us to as Chinese bar. When we got inside it was full of green and white and Celtic gear. We couldn't win.

On the day of the game in Paris we all met up in a pub just off of the main strip. Later on about 40 of us moved off to a bar which was one stop on the metro from the stadium. As it got dark more and more of the boys came in. There was about 70 of us in total with maybe 5 Chelsea boys with us. We had a couple of boys from Middlesbrough with us as well. Ronald, the German, who knows what's going on in the Hooligan Scene all over Europe, was in our company and was trying to get us interested in one of his nutty route marches so as we could find a row. He'd done the same for the Gooners when they were last in Paris playing PS.G. and they'd come unstuck big time by all accounts. I don't know if the French knew we were there but we listened to Ronald or Rommel as he's known to the Chelsea lads, and he led us through the back streets to their main pub. We had no Old Bill with us for ages and then the French Old Bill appeared. They held us for a while and then let us go on our way. Their pub was now just across the road and as I walked towards it our Old Bill appeared and grabbed me. "What you doing"? they asked. "You'll get killed mixing it with this French lot". Next minute our lot who've left me talking to the coppers have come running back after being chased by the French. I could hear it going off but I could do nothing about it as the police had hold of me. I slipped the coppers and we went off down another side road and there was the French mob again. This time we ran at them and they were on their toes. Three times they came back and three times we run them. Then the riot police fired tear gas above our heads and the trouble stopped. The French mob had been attacking Rangers supporters all day and anyone in a Ranger's shirt was being attacked. A lot of our older blokes were being punched and you saw people with bloodied and busted noses. We'd got to their main pub 5 minutes before kick off and apparently half their mob had already left. We'd bumped into 300 or 400 of them but they reckon they had a mob before the game of well over a thousand. I think the French Old Bill thought we were going to get done so they left us to it.

Inside the ground we were in their section and it kicked off with them at half time, about 40 of us stayed in there all through the game. There were lots of stares and threats but it only went off with their stewards.

After the game they held us back and the riot police led us away from the stadium. A few French tried to attack us but got well leathered as even the riot police were fed up with them by this stage and were giving them a few whacks. There was gas and flares used by the French before the game and some were waving their belts about. The Chelsea boys done us proud and were sound. As for that cunt Rommel I don't know what happened to him. I don't think he even threw a punch. On the whole I think we done well out there and I'd give it as a draw.

DEAK

I've been going to Rangers since 1984 and I'm currently on a Banning Order. I've followed Rangers everywhere and had some right rows, but the best one has to be out in Holland when we played P.S.V. Eindhoven in a European game.

Basically we all arranged to meet up in Amsterdam and then got the train through to Eindhoven. There was a good 40 or 50 guys and we'd had contact with one of theirs on the mobile, but they made it clear they wouldn't come to us if the bulk of the Rangers' fans were there.

We got off the train and headed for the stadium. Along the way there was barriers manned by the Dutch police checking that we had tickets. About 30 of us didn't have tickets so the police told us to go back to the town centre as there was no way we would be allowed into the game. We walked off but almost immediately we noticed a few Dutch boys following us and milling around. There was coppers about but they weren't really paying us any attention. Now we were going against the flow of people heading towards the stadium and I just knew it was going to kick off. I just knew that in amongst the public was their mob.

A bit of a disturbance started behind us and we stopped. One of ours asked the youth following us if they were P.S.V. "Yes" said the kid, and then he butted my mate in the face. That was it. It kicked off with just a few of them and the police moved in quickly to break it up. They moved us on until when we got outside the police station then they came from everywhere and surrounded us. There must have been 250 of them and they were all boys and at first it looked a bit dodgy, but then the adrenaline kicked in. We steamed straight into them, which took them by surprise. I knew we were going nowhere because we had the right people there and we were all as game as fuck. It went toe to toe, with the nearest policeman a hundred yards away. They just stood back and watched. They must have thought we were going to get well done. There was camera crews there filming it and I'll swear to God it went toe to toe for minutes. We just kept it tight and didn't budge. We kept backing them off and a few of theirs got decked.

After a while the police pushed us up a side street and then surrounded us and led us out onto the main street until the riot police arrived.

Eighteen of us were jailed for that and all eighteen of us done 3 weeks in a Dutch jail. I was put in the high security prison on my own and

I was told I could end up getting 5 years. I fucking shit myself. They had a special charge for football hooliganism. I got talking to a Dutch guy who was there, and when I told him there was only 30 of us he couldn't believe it. He thought there was hundreds of us. He told me there was 200 Eindhoven and 50 Anderlecht in their firm.

When I was in the prison I watched news reports about the fight. A couple of the guys inside spoke to me about it and they were O.K. I didn't really get any shit while I was in there.

During the court case there was only one witness against us and that was an officer from the Scottish football intelligence Unit. In a statement read out to the court he claimed that he knew everyone before the judge. He told a different story about what he'd seen each of us doing on that night. He told the court he'd seen me punching a guy. He must have had 18 pairs of eyes, plus it was in the dark, so he done well to see us all at the same time misbehaving. Super human or super liar?

My lawyer wanted to question his evidence but we were told that the officer concerned was not in court and his evidence was in the form of a written statement, so my lawyer's request was thrown out of court.

When I was in prison I was feeling pretty low and I questioned myself about all this football hooliganism thing. Was it worth it? How did I get involved? Where was my life going? I was totally pissed off as I stared at the telly in my cell. Then something woke me from my dream-like state as the announcer gave the draw for the European play offs and it was Scotland v England. I jumped up and shouted at the top of my voice "go on you beauty," and I felt fucking brand new again. I was on cloud nine! I felt brand new at the prospect of Scotland v England.

I joined the British National Party (B.N.P.) in 1991 and at one of the meetings I was surprised at just how many people there I knew from football. We've never really had a big immigration problem in Glasgow but over the years that's changed. The I.C.F.- B.N.P. connection came to the fore in Glasgow. We had a fight one Saturday morning with a filthy mob of Celtic and the AFA (Anti-Fascist Action). Six of us steamed into them and sent them running up the road, followed by a couple of burning distress flares. I ended up getting quite high up in the B.N.P. and I even ended up standing in the local elections. When I first joined there was only about 50 members with 30 of them coming from Rangers. Now there are about 200 members and not many coming from football as the B.N.P. cleaned up their image a few years back. I think the ordinary white working class people in this country are just pissed off with politicians and political parties lying to them. They need a voice. They need to be heard. There's nothing wrong in being white and proud of your country is there? It was mainly white British people that fought against Germany in the two World Wars. Some people take a dim view to flying the cross of St. George or the Union Jack from a window or a public building on a specific day. It's just political correctness gone mad. The lunatics have taken over the asylum. I'm no longer a member of the B.N.P. as I've seen them soften their attitudes towards certain things, but I still keep an interest in what's going on.

FAT PAT

Chelsea had two friendlies with Rangers, one down at Chelsea and the other up in Glasgow. When the Rangers fans came down for the game at Chelsea everyone was shaking hands and exchanging scarves and football shirts and whatever. There was a bit of trouble at Earls Court but nothing serious and that game was when the friendship really started.

At the time we had a few right wing boys and so did they, plus we had fans that took the Union Jack flag to games with "Chelsea" emblazoned on it and the Rangers fans being of the same beliefs, used to like that.

For the game up there about 100 of us arrived in Glasgow at 7 0'clock in the morning. One of our lot was selling dodgy £5 notes for £1-50p. We found a pub in the Barrowlands area of the city, which is a predominately Catholic area. The greedy bar owner and his missus were rubbing their hands together with glee as us lot walked in. We had no Old Bill with us and we'd gone undetected since we arrived.

We stayed in there until about midday and the £5 notes were flying over the bar and into the cash till. Old greedy bollocks and his family were loving it. This shit hole had never been as busy and it was taking bundles. That was until one of the lads bought a drink and paid for it with a real £10 pound note and in his change was one of the dodgy fivers. He held it up to the light and had a good look at it. "Here mate," he said to the barman this note's a dodgy one," The governor snatched it out of his hand and held it up to the light giving it a close inspection. The whole pub went quiet. He ran straight to the till to check the rest as a hundred geezers fled from the pub in a bit of a hurry. The story of the dodgy fivers spread like wild fire as the local radio stations, T.V. and newspapers covered the story. No-one would serve us in the shops because as soon as they heard our accents they viewed us with suspicion. We ended up in a few bars over near Ibrox and the Rangers boys couldn't have been friendlier. They loved us. We were singing all the Chelsea and Rangers songs together and it was a great atmosphere.

The one thing they couldn't get over was the size of some of us. We've got some big tall lumps in our firm. Chubby Chris and all his lot knew a lot of the Rangers Casuals so there was no hint of bother.

In the stadium the whole ground sang "We all Agree Rangers and Chelsea are Magic." Everyone was together that night. It's the first time I've ever seen the whole four sides of a ground singing. We used to be like that at Chelsea in the 80s with The Shed, The North Stand, and the West and East Stands all singing together, but this was just different. It made the hair on the back of your neck stand up. It was unbelievable. Most grounds have one end like The Kop or The Stretford End that sing but at Ibrox all four sides of the ground sing and they fucking sing loud and sing their hearts out and they mean it.

A lot of us got put up and spent the night with our new found friends. They didn't know us from Adam but they trusted us to sleep under their roofs. The drinks flowed and a life long friendship was forged. A few of the boys ended up on the piss in an Orange Lodge and it was bingo night so the place was buzzing.

After that Chelsea game quite a lot of the lads started going to a few games up there. They've been up to some of the Rangers v Celtic games and we took a firm up there when Rangers played Aberdeen. Our lot had a right battle with Aberdeen in the ground and cleared them off the terraces. It's a mutual respect between us and Rangers and that still carries on to this day.

The first time I ever met any of the Rangers boys properly down in London was at the Spurs v Rangers friendly at White Hart Lane in 1986. Rangers just ran amok and smashed Spurs everywhere. We had our own little battle outside. There was me, Brains and a drunken Leeds fan called Maz and we fronted about 25 Tottenham boys. We made out we were all carrying weapons and we backed them off. The Old Bill saw what was going on and grabbed hold of us and one of the Spurs fans told the copper I'd been waving around a bottle of squirt. It was in fact a plastic bottle of olibas oil and this grassing

Yiddo was implying it was filled with ammonia. The copper took it off me and had a good look at it; he studied it for a while. "It's only my nasal spray" I told him. "Prove it," he said, and handed it back to me, and like a cunt I held it to one of my nostrils, but before I could give it a gentle squeeze this coppers grabbed hold of it and gave it an almighty squeeze and the contents have shot up my nose and down the back of my throat. Well, it nearly blew my head off as my head almost spun full circle, Exorcist style, and my eyes nearly burst out of their sockets. It came out of everywhere, my nose, my ears, and my mouth. I was coughing and spluttering as the copper and the mob of Yids stood there grinning. "Fuck off," said the copper. "I can't nick ya but serves you right." I never had a cold for 6 months after that and my sinus was clear for another 18 months!

Chelsea were playing Arsenal and Brownie and Smoothie and a few of their other boys came down for the game. After the game about 50 Arsenal slipped their escort but got ambushed on the bridge near The Black Bull pub. A few of the Rangers boys steamed in and earned respect from our lads. Another time we were playing Man Utd and one of our mad boys attacked the United fans with his pet Pit Bull Terrier dog. That day a few of the Rangers lads were with us and again done well. They was also at Kings Cross when we done Leeds after they'd just played at Tottenham and had run the Yids everywhere outside the station. All these things bought the two mobs close.

The funniest one was at Brownie's wedding. A few of our lot went up for it and during the wedding one of the twins' mobile phone started ringing. "That must be Tottenham," someone said and the whole place cracked up!

Over the years I've become a good friend with a lot of them, especially Brownie and Davie who I keep in touch with and class them as real good friends. They're sound fellas and I'm not one for looking into religion. I've got black, white and Asian mates and the colour of someone's skin or religion doesn't bother me. A chap is a chap and a prick is a prick no matter what colour they are. Nice people are nice people; it's as simple as that. At the end of the day I was a football hooligan and I looked at people for what they were not because of their religion or colour. I couldn't give a fuck as long as you're a chap and you're sensible, then you're all right with me. I couldn't give a fuck about your colour or your religion; it just doesn't come into it. It's just a game we all play so let's not cloud it with unnecessary shit.

My old German mate, Ronald, was always talking about just how good the French team, P.S.G.'s mob were. Liverpool or Everton had come unstuck out there. Arsenal had had a rough ride out and done reasonably well on a couple of occasions. So when Glasgow Rangers were due to play in Paris I had to go there. I'd heard that they had huge numbers and that they were well game and that not many teams went there and had a result. I'd also heard that they couldn't be taken lightly so my curiosity got the better of me. I went out there with me mate, Stuart Glass who was celebrating is birthday out there, Gypsy Ben, Muzzer, Jock and a few of the boys from Peterborough. There was about 20 Chelsea out there and a couple of geezers from Man City and Boro, but they wasn't with our firm, they were with the Rangers shirts who unknown to us were getting attacked by a massive, P.S.G.'s firm.

We flew out there and met up in a bar. Me and Ronald the German went up to the ground to get some tickets for the game. A lot of the Rangers' boys didn't like the idea of Ronald being around. The simple fact was Ronald used to go to a few games in Scotland with Hibs. I tried to calm the situation down and said "hang about, Ronald can get us the row and he knows how to find the P.S.G. firm." They gave him a bit of a squeeze and let him know they were leaving it this time but only because of me. He'd been to Paris many times and knew his way around town. It was early doors with no one else around as me and him walked up to the ground, he showed me the route we should take later and showed me the main boozer where their boys, drank.

At the meet later on there was only about 40 of us and to tell you the truth it didn't look too promising. Rangers had taken fifteen thousand fans out there but all their Casuals could muster was 40. We then heard that thousands of Rangers' fans were being attacked in bars up near the ground by a massive mob of P.S.G. Apparently the French had a mob nearly a thousand strong and all they were doing was going from bar to bar and smashing the Jocks. The French Old Bill were doing nothing to stop it but just stood back and let their boys get on with it. As we left the bar we were in, Sandy, one of the main faces at Rangers, got on his mobile to speak to Davie Carrick and told him we were leaving and heading towards the ground.

We got the train and got off one stop before the stadium and met up with Davie and his boys, who were waiting for us. It was now looking a bit better as our numbers had grown to about 80 and it looked like it was 80 good, game fellas. So we set off straight away towards the ground. It was about a half a mile walk to the stadium and everywhere you looked there were Rangers fans decked out in their blue shirts and scarves. We stood out as a Casual firm just by the way we dressed and walked. Divs were coming up to us and were asking where we'd been. "It's over boys," a few blokes with split lips and black eyes said. We've already been done." They told us the French had already been through and had slapped everyone. Someone called those asking for our help, two-faced cunts because the so-called normal supporters in Scotland normally don't have a lot of time for the casuals. We had no Old Bill with us as we strode purposefully through the Parisian streets. We marched off on the route me and Ronald had taken earlier. We were on a long, straight road with side streets running off it and down towards the stadium we could see little groups of blokes walking parallel and trying to keep up with us. "Let's do them," a few of the lads said. "Leave it" was the reply; "we've bigger fish to fry." As we got nearer to the ground we could see the French police moving out of the way of a massive French mob. There was hundreds of P.S.G. heading towards the Rangers end of the ground and now some of the police were running to get out of the way. Our plan was to almost circle the ground and come out on the other side of the stadium and land outside their main pub. Every now and then a small mob of Paris would appear out of a side street but we just ignored them and carried on walking. We were on a mission. We came to a park, which was at the back of their end, which is called `The Kop of Boulogne`. Their boys are supposedly known as `The Boulogne Boys. `

At the top of the road near the ground was a traffic barrier so we stopped, got everyone together and got nice and tight. The old hearts were pumping and the adrenalin was rushing through our veins. "Tonight Mathew, I'm going to be Mike Tyson." I said to myself. We moved off and walked around the metal barrier. Their pub was now on our right and as we got near, their mob appeared. They didn't expect to see us and we steamed straight into them and ran them everywhere. The chant went up "I.C.F. I.C.F." One of the Chelsea lot laughed out loud. "Fuck me, is there West Ham with us?" Next thing it's like firework night as another mob of them have appeared and let go some distress flares into us. A few of them have sprayed gas at us and we've backed off. We've re-grouped and gone at them again, and again they've scattered and seconds later they're back again. This time we've had to turn and run as we were just getting swamped with their huge numbers. Me and Jock from Peterborough were in this side street trying to get our bearings when, what I thought was a distress flare, hit my jacket and bounced off and then hit Jock's jumper, which instantly caught fire. But it wasn't a flare; it was a metal tear gas canister, which had been, fired head height at us by the Old Bill. The whole road filled up with gas and smoke and people were coughing and spluttering. In actual fact that saved our arses because the French couldn't follow us up the road. We caught our breath as the French coppers pushed us up this side road. "Come on lads, we done well there, let's go again," someone said and that seemed to pick everyone up again.

The Old Bill were now behind us so what they'd done is push the French mob into the same street as us. Now the two mobs were facing one another with the Old Bill out of the picture at the back of both firms. I don't know if it was on purpose or just bad policing but we were now walking towards one another. For a minute they looked at us and we looked at them and both firms just couldn't believe it. I called Davie and his boys to the front. "Come on Davie this is your show" I said, so Davie and Sandy rallied their boys. There must have been about 500 French as they came bouncing towards us. We picked up the pace as we walked towards them. You couldn't really pick out or focus on anyone's face in their mob as it was dark but they looked like they meant business. They looked like your average football mob in hooded tops and trainers. "Walk, Walk," came the shout from our side. Suddenly after a few punches, their nerve went and we had them on the move. We ran them about a hundred yards and then they turned and faced us. We stopped and it looked like it could go either way as both mobs bounced up and down in the road. It was a bit of a stand off. Suddenly we took the initiative and stepped into the gap of no mans land and got in amongst them. They were off again and this time the Old Bill came in and stopped it.

As it calmed down a couple of Glasgow Old Bill turned up and advised us not to carry on any more. "What you talking about?" we said, "we've already done them." The Scottish Old Bill looked at one another in disbelief they just couldn't believe we'd actually pulled it off and they almost sounded like they were quite proud of us. They just couldn't believe it. They told us that the P.S.G.mob had even given them a hard time. It had all gone quiet when I spotted a bridge over a river. "Come on," I shouted and ran over this bridge and towards a mob of French on the other side. I soon realized I was on my own and no one else had followed me. The French on seeing this came towards me shouting out something in French, something about me being a fat bastard no doubt. I was back over that bridge in a flash. One of the Rangers lads later said he'd never seen me move so fast and likened me to a Lindford Christie with a weight problem.

Inside the ground I saw Stuart Glass, one of me Chelsea mates, who spotted me in the seats. At the top of his voice he shouts out "I know Pat's prone to exaggeration but his estimation on the size of their mob was a bit conservative to say the least."

When we came out after the game we got together and was escorted away from the stadium. Somehow a mob of about 30 French managed to get in amongst us and they kicked it off. We piled into them before the Old Bill stopped it but give them credit, this little P.S.G. mob were double game. Every road was wet where the Old Bill had cleared their fans from the streets with water cannons.

I rate P.S.G. highly and anyone that plays there should only go there with a top firm. I've since been back there with Chelsea and although we done well we bluffed our way through it out there, and it did come on top for us in the end. To do them over in Paris you'd have to go there with two or three hundred top boys and be prepared to battle. Don't forget you have the Old Bill on their side as well. Ronald did say they have one of the best, if not the best firm in France. They played Marseilles recently in the French Cup Final and it was toe to toe battles in the streets before and after the game. Apparently the two mobs had nearly a thousand strong firm on each side.

To me Chelsea done well out there but I think Rangers, have done the best out of all the British clubs ever to go there. The thing is the French don't travel too well and I've never heard of them coming to England or Scotland or turning up in Belgium or Holland and doing anything. They do turn up like they did at Arsenal and at Chelsea but not with the huge numbers they pull at home. And they keep it very low key almost like they've not looking for trouble. They're not very English like in their travels, abroad. They're what you'd call home-boys.

CHAPTER 8

ENGLISH FIRMS

Elvis Costello once sang that he didn't want to go to Chelsea. I did. I've always had a soft spot for Chelsea. When I was growing up they were the glamour club in England. They didn't win many trophies but to me they were what London was all about. The birds, the booze, the night clubs, the fashion, the Kings Road. Chelsea had it all in abundance. Ossie, Hudson Cooke, they were a team of superstars, plus they've always had that Scottish connection at the club. Tommy Docherty, Charlie Cooke in the 60s and 70s and then came Pat Nevin, Steve Clarke, Joe McLaughlin, Billy Dodds, Kevin McAlister, and plus the Rangers connection with wee Johnny Spencer and Graham Roberts and Danish superstar Brian Laudrup.

The first game I ever went to down at The Bridge was a game with Rangers for the Bradford City Disaster Fund. We took a mob down because we had no idea how it would go or how we'd be received by the Chelsea boys. This was 1985 so there was no real connections between the two sets of supporters. We took a bus down to London for that and a few of the boys went tooled up simply because, as I say, we had no idea how it was going to go.

Before the game we done the usual and went drinking around Trafalgar Square. I don't know what the fascination is between Scotsmen and Trafalgar Square, but it's only us lot and the pigeons that visit it. We moved over to Chelsea and went into a few pubs around near the ground and there were no problems. Everyone was fine. At the stadium we had to go through two lines of police before we got to the turnstile and they were searching everyone so lots of weapons were ditched in the Fulham Road. We went into The Shed end and stood under the old cover. Then the Chelsea fans started singing about hating Celtic so the Rangers' fans around the ground sang the "Spurs Are on Their Way to Auschwitz" song. I think that exchange of songs about each others hated rivals cemented the bond between the two sets of supporters. We'd both found a mutual long lost friend. It was good banter but to my surprise the game wasn't very well attended. There was only just over seven thousand there to see the game end in a 3-2 win for Chelsea.

After the game our firm walked back towards Fulham Broadway station and up in front of us were blue police lights flashing in the darkness. Up ahead was a massive mob. We've all looked at one another. "This is it" I'm thinking and there was a few worried faces in our mob. As we got closer the Chelsea fans standing in the road moved to one side and let us through. As we walked past they cheered and clapped like a guard of honour. A few waved The Red Hand of Ulster flags. It was good. We were made more than welcome.

About 9 months later we played Chelsea at Ibrox in a friendly and lots of the Chelsea boys came up, and again there was no bother. This time we won the game 3-2 in front of seventeen thousand fans. One of my mates from up here, Brownie, had moved down to London and started going to Chelsea, and he got to know a few of the boys so I used to go down and visit him and go to a few games.

We played Hibs at Ibrox and Chelsea bought a few coach loads of boys up for the match. Hibs came up past `The District` pub on Paisley Road West and the Chelsea and Rangers boys piled out of the pub. The Old Bill had the Hibs Casuals wrapped up in a tight escort so you couldn't get near them. One of the Chelsea lads had a flare gun and fired it into the Hibs Mob.

I was down in London when Chelsea played Arsenal and the Gooners mob never turned up so we went drinking over in a pub near Kings Cross, which was owned by Barry Johnstone's mum. As I said before, Barry was one of Rangers' top boys. There was about 50 Chelsea in the boozer and 4 of us from Rangers. One of the boys came into the pub and said that Leeds and Spurs were having it down at the train station, so that was it. The pub emptied and we headed to where the trouble was. By the time we got there Leeds had smashed Tottenham everywhere. The Old Bill were everywhere making themselves busy but that didn't stop the Chelsea boys jumping the metal crash barriers and steaming across the road, at the Leeds Firm, half the Leeds mob ran back into the station while the other half either backed off or stood and fought. The traffic had come to a standstill and the people stuck in their cars looked on in amazement. One of Chelsea's main boys turned to me and asked who, the fuck I was. "I'm Glasgow Rangers" I replied. "All right" he said, and carried on fighting before the police with truncheons broke it up. Chelsea smashed Leeds everywhere and I'd say there was well over 300 Leeds outside that station when we first got there. Chelsea were awesome. As soon as I saw how they performed I was well impressed. They had a top mob out that night. Leeds had just done the Tottenham mob that had turned up at Kings Cross, to give them a farewell present to take back to Yorkshire, so it was a good result for the Chelsea lads.

I was also at Parsons Green with Chelsea when a West Ham fan got stabbed. I saw it. We got pulled in for that. I saw the Old Bill lifting the boy's tee shirt up and seeing how bad it was. West Ham had come across the green towards us lot who were in a pub across the other side of the green. It went gone toe to toe for a while. A few flares were then fired into the West Ham mob and they then bolted. It was a little scary for a bit and then it turned Chelsea's way. I was standing on the edge of the green with a bottle in my hand and a copper pulled up sharp on his motor bike. He was going that fast he swerved and fell off. That was it, we were off and the Old Bill chased after us. We went past the pub we'd just left and I heard a copper shout "Stop Stop." "Yea Righto" I'm thinking "I'm off". As I got to the end of the road a van full of Old Bill pulled up in front of us. I was fucking knackered and was about to give up anyway. They questioned me about the stabbing and then let me go.

I went with Chelsea to a game over at Tottenham and we met up in a pub in North London at 9 o'clock in the morning. It was somewhere over near Enfield. We came down with an Aberdeen boy who went with Tottenham. He got us some dodgy tickets for the train down. After the game the police rounded a lot of the Chelsea mob up and chucked us onto a double Decker bus and drove us around London. A few of the lads started getting the hump and kicked up a bit of a fuss about being driven about so the police stopped the bus and threw us all off. We all made our way back to a pub over near Victoria and as we got there the boy from Aberdeen phoned me to tell me Spurs were coming to the pub. I told everyone but no one would listen. "They won't come" lots of them said, "they're full of shit". Loads started drifting off into the night pissed off by the magical mystery tour on the bus.

It was about 11 o'clock at night and Tottenhams firm turned up. There was about 25 of them and the same number of us and it went fucking mental in the middle of the street. My mate, Ricky, got done down the side of the head by a big darkie. It was a good fight until the Old Bill turned up and we all disappeared. From what I've seen of Tottenham they didn't have that good a mob but nowadays a few people rate them and by the sound of it they've got a lot better. As I said, they've got a big thing with Aberdeen.

A couple of our boys have been down to London with Millwall and a few of theirs have been up to Ibrox. I went to Millwall to watch them play Middlesbrough because my mate played for the Boro. After the game I was in the players' lounge at the back of the stand and as we came out the police were leading a mob of Millwall out of the ground past us. They looked a good outfit and there was about 300 of them. They'd been sitting in the seats just looking menacing. I later spoke to a few of the Boro boys who said they had no chance against this nutcase, Millwall firm.

The team I don't rate in London is Arsenal. Their mob's proper shite. We played them in a friendly five or six years ago and the game was only announced 3 days before so none of our boys went down for it. Our support was all kids and Scarfers but that didn't stop Arsenal from slapping a few Rangers about. They took liberties that day and they know it.

With West Ham I haven't really seen a lot of them first hand. I saw them with Chelsea at Parsons Green but West Ham's reputation goes before them. The I.C.F. were legendary up and down the country and they were organized like an army so you have to respect what they've done in the past.

When I was a kid Rangers played down at Aston Villa in a mid-season friendly in 1976. Thousands of Rangers' fans headed to Birmingham, many arriving early in the morning and by lunch time had drunk the pubs dry. There was untold trouble and a couple of people were treated for stab wounds. At the game Rangers' fans tried to storm into the Holte End, which was the massive terrace behind the goal where the home fans stood. With Rangers leading 2-0 the game had to be abandoned after a pitch invasion. There was over 100 arrested with widespread condemnation from the press, both in England and in Scotland. Many asked the question who in their right minds had organized such a game? Some papers even claimed the trouble was caused by Rangers' fans being anti Catholic and venting their feeling on the Villa fans. What a load of bollocks. We were playing Aston Villa not Glasgow Celtic. This was nothing to do with religion. It was a Scottish team playing an English team. Work it out for yourselves and you don't have to be a politician or a journalist or a priest or a vicar to come up with the answer.

I remember watching the news reports at home on our old black and white telly. Part of it showed a football special pulling out of Birmingham's New Street Station with kids hanging out the smashed windows waving their Rangers' flags and scarves. "Bloody Hooligans" said my mum. I smiled. Some of the kids hanging out of the train only looked about the same age as me. I was a bit envious I wasn't there with them. I've always had a bit of a nose for trouble.

Over the years the older lads have spoken about that trip to Birmingham so I've heard first hand accounts of what went on. The same as our victory in the European Cup Winners Cup Final in Barcelona over Russian side Dynamo Moscow in the early 70s. Estimates put the Rangers support at well over thirty thousand. Even in victory our fans caused a riot with pitch invasions, bottles covering the pitch and with claims of opposing players being assaulted and the armed Spanish police being chased off the pitch and out of the ground. Imagine if we had of lost?

We played Chesterfield in, I think it was, the Old Inter City Fairs Cup, which is now the UEFA Cup. Fuck knows how Chesterfield qualified for that but I remember they bought about three thousand fans up to Ibrox and they got smashed everywhere.

In '97 we played Everton at Goodison for Dave Watson's testimonial. We took a bus down there and met up with a few other boys so there was about 70 of us in a couple of pubs in Liverpool city centre. There was a few Scousers in there that looked like their boys. Their numbers grew to about 20 or 30 of them and they were right cheeky fuckers. Half a dozen of us left the pub we were in, and this group of Scousers were standing around outside. An argument started and it looked like they were going to try and take a few liberties but before it kicked off the rest of our boys piled out of the pub across the road. Punches were thrown and the Scousers were on their toes. A few of them got caught and were getting leathered. The Old Bill turned up and I was arrested and handcuffed and thrown on the deck. A Scottish copper from Falkirk came over and advised me not to play up and to keep my mouth shut. "These boys don't fuck about so be careful," he warned, and with that I was taken in the back of a van to the police station. When I got inside I couldn't believe what was gong on. Rangers' fans were being physically dragged in through the main doors and thrown against the charge desk and any complaints about the Old Bill's behaviour was met with a battering with their truncheons. Whilst all this was going on a copper was stood behind the charge desk doing his paper work. He didn't look up once and was oblivious to what was going on around him. I was charged with a breach of the peace and taken off to be finger printed and photographed. The bloke doing the finger prints was a fellow Scot and told me he was putting in a complaint about the police as to the way they were treating the Rangers' fans. "They're bang out of order what they're doing to you's lot" he said. As I was being released with a few of the others, a Rangers' fan, who was dressed in a suit, was being spoken to at the charge desk. It turns out this man was a lawyer from Glasgow. He complained that he'd never seen such treatment in the whole of his life. The police were brutal and that's an under-statement.

I was released at 11 o'clock at night, just in time to make the bus back to Glasgow. The boys told me that before the game about 60 of ours went around the back of Everton's end and had a row with about 60 to 70 of them and done them all over the place.

After that game and seeing Everton's mob first hand I don't rate them at all. They talk a good fight but there's lots more English teams I rate above them.

One such team is Bradford City. We took a bus load down there for ex-Rangers and Bradford City player, Stuart McCall. It was a testimo-nial game, not against Rangers but a team made up of ex-pros from different clubs, but it was still a full house. We met in a pub in the town centre and our mob that day was 150 strong. It was a good turn out. We got a police escort to the ground and we never saw a Bradford firm but we heard on the grapevine that they were up for it and would be turning out for us. Twenty of us gave the Old Bill the slip up near the ground and went into a pub. A mate of mine gave me a call on the mobile and said because the game was poor they'd decided to leave. As they've left the ground a mob of Bradford have appeared armed with bottles and pool cues and tried to set about them. The Old Bill have stepped in before it's kicked off and the Bradford firm have fucked off. We've done no more than left the pub and gone looking for this Bradford firm. We met up with those leaving the ground and now we had a nice tight, 40 handed firm. We hunted around for them and found them in a pub but as soon as they've seen us coming towards them they've come to the doors armed with pool cues. We've smashed every window in the pub and steamed the doors but they wouldn't come out. Within minutes the police have come and rounded us up and start escorting us into town. Next minute we've 50 Bradford coming up the street behind us. The next thing is they've cut up a side street and come out in front of us in an entrance to a shopping precinct and now they're facing us. They come towards us and their Old Bill are allowing them to come towards us. We've got 4 or 5 Glasgow football Old Bill with us who tell us to get moving or we're nicked. Our coppers were trying to get us up a side street and out of the shopping centre but the Bradford coppers just stood back knowing its about to go. Bradfords firm have run at us and come into us with fists and boots flying. They had a black lad and a half caste lad at the front of their firm who were as game as fuck. I was quite surprised that most of their mob were white. I thought being Bradford they'd have had quite a few Asians in their firm. Perhaps if it had of been cricket then it would have been a different story. A few of our lads had grabbed hold of some scaffolding poles and fittings from a nearby building site but that didn't stop them or back them off. I'll give Bradford their due, they were good and were as game as fuck. It was one nasty row. It went toe to toe. One of our coppers stood back and filmed it and on the video which I've seen you can see these metal scaffolding clips flying through the air. One of his mates grabbed me and he was panicking, "Davie, what the fuck are you doing?" he asked, his face ashen white. "What do you want me to do?" I replied. I was just about to launch one of these scaffolding fittings towards the Bradford mob when he held onto my throwing arm. It was like the Battle of Agincourt with bricks, bottles and bits of metal raining down from the skies. It was only spoilt by more Old Bill arriving on the scene. It was probably one of the best rows I've ever been involved in at football. And no one from either side took a backwards step. It was brilliant.

We played Bradford's near neighbours, Leeds, in the Champions League a few seasons back with both clubs banning one another's travelling support. There was no trouble really at both games. With both mobs not travelling a few Rangers' fans even bought season tickets at Elland Road purely to watch the Rangers game down there. We turned out for them up here but we heard from a few boys up here that go with the Leeds firm that they would not be coming.

When they played Celtic up here they turned out a top mob, about 30 of us lot joined up with about 400 Leeds. We walked past a Celtic pub and it was packed to the rafters with Leeds' lads. They were all right with us and they accepted us. They were brilliant. We showed them the back way to the ground and came out at The Gallowgate. We walked past a few pubs and one of the Leeds lads stopped and opened the doors to a pool hall and standing there, looking back at us, was John O`Kane, who is one of Celtic's main boys and a right liberty taker as well. He tried it on with me once. I'd gone into a pub to meet someone for a drink and for something to eat before a Rangers v Celtic game and this cunt Caine and his mates from the lefty mob Red Action are sitting in there. Caine got up and walked over to me. "Davie, we can do this the easy way or the hard way" he says. "What are you talking about you daft cunt?" I replied, and with that he's tried to stick the nut on me. I've hit him with a bottle and he's gone down. The rest of them have thrown bottles and bar stools at me and soaked me with drink. The thing is the drink thrown at me hit the rest of the customers in there more than it got me. There was a kitchen door so I went through it and pulled that shut. These stupid cunts couldn't open it. All I had after all that was a boot mark on my chest but a few of them had cut heads and bruises. So when I saw this liberty taking cunt inside the doorway of that pool hall he had to have it. I hooked him with a perfect shot. A few of the Leeds boys went steaming in through the doors but were beaten back by cunts with pool cues. The Celtic boys inside wouldn't come out as the doors were kicked in and the windows smashed. 400 Leeds fans stood outside there in the road singing "No Surrender to the I.R.A." It was brilliant. It made the hairs on the back of my neck stand up. I've never heard it sung with so much venom.

We played Sunderland in 93 down there in a friendly. We took two bus- loads of boys down there and got drinking in a pub in the town centre. It was a dark old pub with a downstairs part to it. There'd been no trouble and everyone was spread out having a few beers. Next minute five Sunderland lads have come in and started getting a bit cheeky with a few Rangers' fans with shirts on who were just sitting there having a drink. It was dark in there so these five didn't have a clue how many of us were drinking in the shadows and down-stairs. They started getting a bit more mouthy and a few of ours had heard enough and got stuck into them. They tried to get away but got caught on the stairs and one of them was cut down the face. Another boy was caught outside and he was cut as well. We fucked off up towards the ground and the Old Bill tried blocking our way with a line of men, some with police dogs. Behind the line of coppers was Sunderland's mob shouting abuse and calling us on for a fight. We went straight through the Old Bill and had the Sunderland mob on its toes.

We got to the ground and there was more scuffles. There was a big bit in the national papers about these two Sunderland fans that were slashed. The papers claimed they were innocent. Like fuck were they, they were two of their main boys who were out to cause trouble and they came unstuck. I did hear that the Rangers' supporters club had invited them up as their guests and that the two of them were given season tickets as a goodwill gesture.

Many years later we played them in a friendly up here and the word on the street was that Sunderland were coming and that they were out for revenge. We got a good mob out and we waited for them but never saw them all day. We were well up for it. One of ours saw some of their mob in the game, so we knew they were about. At 11 o'clock at night they phoned us and told us to meet them in Duke Street. We only had 25 boys left as everyone else was away home. I thought it was a wind up and I told everyone that they wouldn't be there. Anyway, we jumped in a few cars and a couple of taxis and made our way over to where they said they were and sure enough, there they was. They were about 40 handed drinking in `The Bristol`, which is a known Loyalist pub. Apparently the boys working behind the bar in there gave them crates of empty bottles to use as ammo against us. The Bristol is a fucking Rangers pub so what these cunts were playing at I don't know. One of our boys, Colin, had a baseball bat and fired straight into them. One of theirs had armed himself with a scaffold pole and he's caught Colin in the face with it and nearly took his eye out. It went on for 10 minutes with battles up and down the street. Those that went down got whacked good and proper. We were knackered but we managed one last charge and had them on their toes. A few got caught and 9 of them got taken to hospital. There was no one to my knowledge arrested on the night. By the time the Old Bill came it was finished. I rate Sunderland after that battle. They were very good and performed well.

We played Irish team, Shelbourne, in a Cup game but the game was moved to Tranmere Rovers' ground. Why that was the choice of venue, I've no idea. I don't think they'd let us play at Shelbourne for obvious reasons. So for Shelbourne this was their home leg. No one from them turned up at Ibrox, just a few supporters, and no sign of any Celtic mob. A lot of the boys went down for the game at Tranmere and it kicked off down there, not with Shelbourne or Tranmere, but with a load of scumbags off of a council estate, but Tranmere ain't too far from Merseyside and Liverpool have that bit of a connection with Celtic, but personally I don't think its as big as some people make out. All right, there's the Kenny Dalglish thing and there's a big Irish community living there but do Scousers really give a shit about Celtic? Plus, there's the flute bands and the annual Orange parades held in Liverpool. Nowadays there's probably more Afro-Caribbean and Asian people in Liverpool than there are Catholics.

The first time we played Man Utd I was only a young kid but the trip down to Manchester is still spoke about by some of our older lads who were boys in their time. We took thousands down there and just took the piss. The ground was a sea of blue and white and any United silly enough to stand and fight were battered. Afterwards everyone went back into the city centre and took over every pub and bar. United were humiliated on their own patch with the old saying ringing in their ears that there's always someone bigger and tougher than you.

Fast forward nearly 30 years and the Mancs got their long awaited revenge. There were over six thousand fans from Manchester for a Champions League game in Glasgow with their main firm totalling over 400 and I'll give them their due, they were well organized and took over many of Rangers' bars and pubs. We just couldn't seem to get our act together that night and for some reason our organization was a total shambles. But I'll give United their due, they came looking for it and you can't take that away from them,
Manchester police were involved with the making of a TV documentary and it showed the superintendent telling the cameras that news had just come in that there was a group of people traveling down from Scotland for that weekends Manchester derby. He added that this group had been detained by his officers on the platform, but no sooner had he said that then you could see two of the Rangers boys on the telly walking behind him. We caught the train down to Preston and as we went to change for the Manchester train the place

was swarming with old bill, I tried kidding on I wasn't with the rest of the lads and walked away but the old bill sussed it. " Mr Carrick can I have a word with you" one of them said. They told us they were keeping an eye on us and not to cause any trouble. We left the station and had a beer and then caught the train to Manchester. When we got there the old bill was again waiting for us and penned about twenty of the boys in with dogs. I again tried to give them the slip and tried putting on a Manc accent "Who does Robert Carlyle think he is? Smiled the copper, as he put me in with at all the boys surrounded by his colleagues. A few of the Hibs boys came down that day and joined up with United and they were with them when City smashed them There was 35 of the Rangers boys down for that game and we drank around Moss Side with all the City boys who treated us well.

Portsmouth's mob is another firm I rate down south. I was in London when they played Liverpool in the F.A. Cup semi final at Highbury and me and a few Chelsea faces were having a drink in a West End pub when 70 Pompey lads came in and had a look around. A few of them knew Tony C from Chelsea who was sitting with us. It kicked off in the street with Liverpool and Pompey later on in the day but from what I saw of them they have a decent mob.

JOCK

I'm now 37 years old and have lived for all but 4 years of my life in Peterborough. I was born in Glasgow but moved south with my mum and dad when I was a kid. I've followed `The Posh`, my home-town team. We've always had a good mob and for some games years ago, we could pull anything from 150 to 200 boys when we played the likes of Cambridge or Northampton. They were our main rivals. Now we could perhaps pull 40 on a good day.

When I was about 14 I saw Chelsea and Sunderland playing in a Cup game at Stamford Bridge. I was down the local youth club and watched it on the telly. I also heard reports of all the trouble on the news and saw it in the papers the next morning. So I thought to myself "that's the team for me".

My dad's in the Orange Order and was a big Rangers' fan. He was from Coatbridge, which is just outside Glasgow. Work took my mum and dad to Peterborough so I've always followed Rangers. I used to have all the players' pictures up on my bedroom wall. My favorites at the time were Gazza, Graham Roberts and Terry Butcher. Now Martin King reckons the only posters I have on my bedroom walls are of Wayne Sleep, Freddie Mercury and George Michael. (Joke) I was a big Rangers' fan even before I started following Chelsea. I've never been up to a Rangers' game with any of the Chelsea lads. The only time I've been to a game up there was with Davie Carrick who I met on Brooney's stag do in Blackpool.

I went to see a Rangers v Celtic game but it was shit as we lost 2-0, but for atmosphere it was untouchable. There's no game in the world that could beat it. It was unbelievable. I never saw any trouble inside or outside the ground but there was trouble in Glasgow that night. The mob of Rangers I was with stumbled across a pub full of Celtic fans and it kicked off. It went mental and there was bottles, glasses and ashtrays flying through the air and people crashing through the windows. It was like a Wild West cowboy film.

Rangers seem to be the better organized firm who dress better and carry themselves better, whereas Celtic dress and act like a load of pikeys or gypsies.

Over the years I've never really been able to afford to go to many games up there so I've been a bit of an armchair fan, like most Man

Utd. fans I suppose. Financial restrictions and marriage have stopped me going to more games up there but I've always been Rangers through and through. I think the relationship between Rangers and Chelsea fans is fantastic. Just look at that turn out for the Celtic game at Stamford Bridge recently. Rangers were well represented. It was like turning the clock back 20 years. Don't forget the game was in midweek, yet all those fans traveled down from Scotland to follow Chelsea and they deserve a big pat on the back, well done lads you done us proud. There was people kicking about from all over the place. You had Alloa, Airdrie, Hearts, Rangers, and Dundee who all came down to support Chelsea. As I say, it was like the old days.

It just shows that the football hooligan is alive and kicking. That night against Celtic was more important than football to some people and at times it showed. The only way to stop trouble at football is to lock everyone up aged 13 to 75 and then that might stop it. I think looking smart at football is all about looking good, not like that Celtic mob the other night they looked like Swampy, the New Age Traveller. They looked like they were off to liberate a load of rabbits from a testing centre, the scruffy cunts.

CHAPTER 9

CHARLIE CHANG

I've had my problems with the glue sniffing as a youngster but as long as I can remember drugs have played a big part in most peoples' lives up here. When I was 15 or 16 it was the amphetamine (speed) and the L.S.D. (acid) that was fashionable. At the time I was never really into the weed and the puff. It just never appealed to me. I've been to football on a Saturday still out of my nut from the Friday night. I think drugs crossed over into football fans' lives when the rave scene started. Before that it was Hippies that smoked dope and dropped acid and downers and speed. But the rave scene opened up a whole new way of life for lots of people.

I've heard it said that it killed organized football violence for a few years, and that may well be true. The music and the drugs and the love and peace thing was everything that the hardcore Casuals just didn't stand for but it's surprising how ya life can change after you've dropped a few Es. One minute you was punching the fuck out of a rival fan and the next you were dancing with him. Sweating ya bollocks off in a muddy field or a disused warehouse in flared trousers, Kicker boots and a loud flowered shirt, drinking bottles of water at £10 a go. What was that all about? And the music. You could get a better tune out of an angle grinder. I bet some of these cunts could cringe when they look back but the people that organized these raves were making bundles. Money definitely talked. You'd get the faces from different casual firms, who normally hated one another with a passion, come together to promote these events. It didn't matter what club you supported, if there was a pound note to be earned your diffences for the time being were put to one side. This was the sad face of football.

With Rangers we'd go to somewhere like Hibs for a game and all we'd take through there was maybe 20 boys. Lots of our lot would have been out on the Friday night and the next morning still be full of acid and couldn't get up for the game. The Es made everyone loved up and all that bollocks. I just couldn't get into it. I hated the music. It was like something the Germans or the Spanish would dance to on holiday. It was cheap, crappy music. It used to annoy me because I could see it fucking up our mob. A few of us stuck with the football for a few years and to tell you the truth if we hadn't we would have, God forbid ended up like Celtic with no mob, or even struggling to put a mob together. Even for those all-important games, which meant so much to so many people.

I remember getting talked into going to one of these raves and there was a coach load of Hibs boys there and about 30 or 40 of Airdrie's Section B, turned up. There was only four of us there and two of them were Celtic fans, but no one gave us any grief or said anything. They knew who we were but they were all loved up and were only there to do their robotic dancing under the flashing strobe lights. For some strange reason it didn't appeal to me to drive hundreds of miles and then pay a tenner to get in and dance like a mong in a muddy field with cows shit half way up your knees.

Nowadays cocaine is a well-established part of football culture. It's imbedded in the scene. It goes hand in hand with most of the mobs. We went up to Aberdeen on a coach for an away game, which one of our boys was running, on board we had a couple of Cardiff boys with us for the trip. One of our lot had a big bag of coke with 28 grams inside. The Cardiff lads thought that we were taking some of it up for the boys we were meeting up there. The boys on the coach did the whole bag before we reached Perth, the whole stash was used up and gone just an hour and a half into the journey. The Welsh boys couldn't believe it.

Coke plays a big part in football now and there's also a lot of money to be made. The police must know it's going on. I did hear a story that after one home game a couple of coppers came into the pub and had a few beers after they'd come off of duty. One of them got half canned and started talking to a few of the lads. He said that the Old Bill weren't interested in our cocaine habits but were really only interested in us behaving ourselves and not over stepping the mark. They knew that coke was being taken on a regular basis but it seems they were willing to turn a blind eye to some peoples habit. They weren't interested in dealing with the drugs, it seems they were only making themselves busy on keeping tabs on the mob. Saying that though the police have been in the pubs with sniffer dogs in the past looking for drugs.

When we were up in Aberdeen once the Old Bill held us in a pub and began searching everyone. They found grams of coke, knives, puff, you name it, but our boys discarded it, down the backs of seats and under tables and down the toilet before the Old Bill found it in their possession. You could have opened a chemist with the amount of pills that were stuffed down the back of the chairs or tucked under the carpet. It's all part of football now and it's also a major part of society. It was once many years ago the designer drug of the rich and famous, but over the last 10 years it's become more readily available even though it's far too expensive for what it is. You can pay thirty, forty to fifty pound a gram for it and most of it is cut to fuck with one thing or another. Babies teething powder, hay fever tablets, water retention tablets and even rat poison are just a few of the things Ive heard being used to cut the cocaine with. You won't be getting much chang for ya money, that's for sure, but saying that it does depend on who you buy from.

We have a few boys who come with our firm who have made lots of money through the drugs. I think it's the same all over the country and then down south you get a few people making even more money by selling the snide designer gear they make more money from the hooky clothes then they would from selling drugs. Up here you wouldn't last 5 minutes wearing a snide Lacoste or Stone Island top at football. It would get spotted straight away and you wouldn't get away with it. You'd never be allowed to live it down. You'd have the piss taken out of you non-stop.

Glasgow is a tough City and a tough place to live. It's always had this certain reputation of the razor gangs and the Billy Boys and the gangsters, and it has within it tough areas as well. Most people have heard of The Gorbals and its' violent reputation. No Mean City, a book and a film about Glasgow's razor gangs set in the 1930s, was one attempt to portray the underbelly of Glaswegian society. Glasgow has even been voted as the European City of Culture. Fucking hell, that must have took some doing! You still have the crime families in the city that run things. It's mostly done by area. One family will run the show in a certain part of the city. Catholic and Protestant will work together. When it comes to money there's no such thing as religion.

The big thing up here is running the security on building sites. How it works, is quite simple if someone's building new houses or flats or apartments then a member of the gang will speak to the builders and tell them that the security for the site will be done by so and so and it will cost the builder x amount of pounds a week to make sure everything runs smoothly and that theres no break-ins or thefts. If they agree everything's fine. If they don't then there's a possibility that the site could get burnt down. It's as simple as that. The builder pays for the site to be protected and everyone's happy.

Other families do the doors on the pubs and clubs, and others, the drugs. We've had a few dooremen come with the mob in the past. Some even got in trouble with one of the big Sunday papers that ran a story about the bouncers selling drugs to punters in a Glasgow city centre pub. We used a pub called The John Street Jam, which for a while was the in place in Glasgow. It was very trendy and was full of our firm and loads of pretty women. The paper accused the bouncers of selling drugs but what was really happening was that one of our boys was making a nice few quid by supplying everyone. So they were nearly right.

I think Glasgow is still as bad as it's ever been. You still get people getting slashed and cut but now you're getting more shootings. Every week you hear of someone being shot and killed and in one week recently in Glasgow there were 3 people shot and killed. It's so easy to get a gun in Glasgow. There's people who can get you one within half an hour. It'll cost you anything from £300 to £700 depending on what you want and if you use it. You can buy a gun outright for a slightly cheaper price, a sort of rental but if you use it you have to pay the full price. Lots of people tend to rent one and just keep it on them for protection. You can buy a good handgun for £600 and it's yours to keep.

A few people carry C.S. gas or pepper spray on them but that ain't a lot of good against a bullet. A few of the boys go across to France and bring it back. It's legal over there and can be found in the shops easily. In the papers recently they ran a story about a batch of electronic cattle prods being delivered to someone up in Glasgow. A few of the gangsters got hold of them and they're that powerful they can knock you off ya feet and spark out. They say if you've got a dodgy heart it could even kill you. They've got sort of prongs on them sticking out. They're really sort of stun guns.

In Glasgow now we have a big immigration problem. In the last 10 years you have these Eastern Europeans settling up here and with it they've bought their own ways of making money. They've tried muscling in on the drugs trade and prostitution but they get nowhere because the people that have run it up her for years are too heavy. So there's no way they'd get a foothold in Glasgow. The Chinese and the Triads do their own things and nay bother anyone else. They don't tread on anyone's toes.

I think some of the players we have at Rangers now must be on the gear, because they're that bad. Some of them are on thirty grand a week but they should be paying us to watch them. Over the last few years we've reduced the wage bill at the club and we no longer pay silly money for wages. Gone are the days of paying of 50 – 60 – 70 grand a week. Most of that was spent on mediocre players who were just there for the money. I think we've had every nationality in the world pull on the Rangers' jersey, most of them, shit.

Leeds tried it a few years back in an attempt to win the Champions League and buy success. They paid out fortunes in wages and on transfers. They flung money at players and it went pear shaped and they nearly went under and that was a wake up call to all clubs, including Rangers. Before it was too late we woke up and took notice.

I think the paying public would agree there are far too many prima donnas in football these days. Getting back to the drugs thing I think some of the players off field activities and some of their social lives may well affect their performances on the pitch. There's always rumours doing the rounds up here about certain players with certain habits and a few names constantly crop up. I won't name names but most people who follow football in Scotland will have their own ideas as to who's at it. Every club has 2 or 3 players that like to social-ize a bit on the heavy side and are partial to a bit of the old Charlie Chang. Well so rumour 'as it.

BORIS

I started going with the Rangers mob in the mid 90s. I was about 18 or 19 but I'd been around the periphery of things from a young boy.

I came from Deniston, which is a rough area of Glasgow and is an I.C.F. stronghold. When I was 14 I tagged along with a mob of Rangers and went over to a game at Parkhead.

In '97-'98 I went with the Scottish National Firm to a few games and then I progressed on into going with the Rangers firm. In them days the main faces were Davie and Billy Britain and there was a hardcore of 40 to 50 of us that went everywhere. We kept it really tight and we didn't let just anybody in with us. I could tell you everybody name by name in that firm at the time that's how tight we were. Not being big headed but we used to do really well. It wasn't often that we'd get turned over.

I started going just at the right time. I got my foot in the door because I used to go with the East End firm on a supporters' bus to away games, and a big part of that bus were in the I.C.F. I went to games in Belgium and France. I was a young kid and my face seemed to get known and the older lads knew I was game and I wouldn't hesitate to back them up when it kicked off.

The best row I've ever had following Rangers was when we played P.S.V. in Holland. I was one of them arrested and put in the jail. Paris St Germain was another top row in 2001. Every time we have a game out in Europe there's all sorts of English boys turn out, but that just shows the Britishness of Rangers. The P.S.V. game was when I'd say the I.C.F. were at its height. We had a tight, good firm and on that night in Holland we proved just how good we were.

The thing is in Scotland the hooligan scene is still going strong. A lot of the teams are now pulling mobs together. A lot of the so-called smaller clubs are now getting 40 or 50 lads together. Aberdeen have still got a hardcore mob but it's always been hide and seek with them. They have 3 or 4 good game lads and the rest are just total piss heads that want to jump up and down in the road and have a row with you in front of the police. That's why they've never been to Glasgow and done it. Aberdeen's that far up the road that by the time they get to Glasgow they're that well oiled they're too pissed to do anything.

Hibs are another mob who talk a good fight. We played them in the 4th round of the Cup and they were on the phone weeks before the game telling us they were coming through with 150 lads. We got a meet organized with them for 9.30 on the morning of the game on the outskirts of Glasgow City Centre. The buzz went around our lads and the feeling was that this was going to be the one. We turned out massive but what did they do? They turned up 15 minutes before the game on two coaches that parked right outside the ground. "What's the crack?" we asked them. "You've been bigging it up all week". They came out with all the usual shite, claiming they were the Hibs young lot. They said their older mob were coming later. That told us everything. We went there a couple of seasons back 100 handed, and with no Old Bill we went straight into their main boozer, but there was only a handful of them in there. I'll give Hibs their due, since I've been going to football Hibs have always had a top mob but in the last few years they ain't too keen to mix it with us.

The best firm in Scotland now is the Old Bill. No one can touch them. They've fucked everyone over the last few years.

It's not just about fighting at football, it's also about looking good and fashion plays a big part in the scene. I'd much rather someone next to me who ain't going nowhere, in a pair of Dr. Martens and a ripped jumper and jeans than someone in a Stone Island jumper that can't fight and runs off before a punch is thrown. Believe me, there's plenty of them about. They stand at the end of the road watching in their £400 Stone Island jacket while you get a good doing. You always want your boys to look smart but not at any price.

The scruffiest mob has to be Celtic ain't it? Celtic ain't a football firm, they're a scruffy street gang. Rangers, Hearts, Hibs and Aberdeen are all football firms but not fucking Celtic. They don't move from the Gallowgate. They don't travel anywhere. They won't come past Glasgow Cross. They stick to their bit and don't move. They drink in their Paddy pubs which all have cameras and C.C.T.V. so they know they're safe.

We bumped into them three or four years' back at The Merchant City and we legged them everywhere, as soon as it went toe to toe they were off. In ten years that's the first Celtic mob I've ever seen and I'll bet it'll be another ten or more before I see another one.

CHAPTER 10

AIN'T MISBEHAVING?

I've been arrested for various things at football 16 or 17 times, and I've been to court for these offences 16, 17 times. I've been held in prison on remand twice. I done 110 days in Barlinie for the Scotland v England game. That turned a bit political with the English papers screaming for blood because they said one of theirs had come up to see the game and he was a decent fan, so they said, and he ended up sustaining a serious injury. They claimed he'd been attacked by a Scottish thug. Next thing the Home Office got involved in it and they asked for a month's extension to my remand. I ended up doing 4 months on remand and was taken to court and then I got a not guilty.

The second bit of prison was incurred at a match against Motherwell. I got a week lay down in Barlinie. This procedure enables the police to get their case together in 7 days before they fully commit you or let you go free. After 7 days you go up in front of the prosecutor and put your case across. The Old Bill do the same, then the prosecutor decides if you're given bail or held in remand. My lawyer done well and won my case and I was let out after a week on bail. It ended up going to the high court where I was found guilty of various charges. I'd been arrested for fighting with Motherwell fans and I was done for a serious assault. The case against me for cutting a Motherwell boy with a knife was dropped. But they done me for an offensive weapon and I was also done for a breach of the peace. I was sentenced at the high court in Edinburgh and I got community service. Did I get off light or what? I worked in old folks' home where I made them cups of tea and toast. It was a heavy punishment. Every night after I finished at work I'd go there for 3 hours at a time and help out. I done that for 6 months but I really enjoyed it. They were a nice bunch of people. Lots of them started coming to Rangers with me on a Saturday and they were a right nasty little firm. No, not really, just pulling your pisser!

I lived with a lassie for 7 years and then I met someone else and was with her for 15 years. We then split up so I headed down south just to get away from everything. Up here drink and drugs and violence surrounded me and I just needed to get my head together and have a re-think and sort out in which direction my life was going. I'd basically had enough of everything.

I got myself a job and done well and kept out of trouble but I missed my kids. My boy is 18 and my wee girl is 9. He knows all about my past and about everything I've done at football. I took him down to a Man City v Tottenham game and we met all the City boys and had a few too many beers so a couple of the City boys put us up in one of the top hotels in Manchester. It was a good day and he really enjoyed himself.

There's a big connection with Rangers and Man City. My brother's a keen City fan and quite a few of them come up for games at Ibrox. I think the connection comes from Celtic's affiliation with Man Utd so because of our dislike of all things Celtic we look out for City's results. So maybe it's a bit to do with that, plus United have always been the glamour club and City the underdog so we favour the underdog. Manchester's like Glasgow with the rivalry between two clubs. Plus Man City have quite a few Loyalists in their ranks.

At the Tottenham game we were at, there was a massive big flag in the crowd behind us and it had on it the R.A.F. symbol, like a target and written on it was Man City and Glasgow Rangers. They've got some good boys who treat us with the utmost respect.

Thirty five of us went down there when they beat Man Utd 4 – 1 and outside City ran United's firm everywhere. In the pub afterwards they had a right nasty looking firm who was well over a 150 strong. When we played United up here in the Champions League they bought about 400 boys, most of them dressed in black. Fuck knows what that's all about. Our boys were split up all over Glasgow that night but about 15 of us made a stand against them in Paisley Road West and a few of them came into us and we exchanged punches before the police moved us on. It went off again at the ground behind the Copeland Road stand and we give it to a few of them and the rest of them backed off. Lots of them were steaming drunk as they'd been in the city since early morning. For the game down there we took about 60 boys, that was purely down to the lack of tickets allocated to Rangers.

On the day of the game the Manchester Old Bill closed all the bars and pubs so we couldn't get a drink anywhere. We were well pissed off, that was until Man City fan, Micky Francis, saved the day and found us a pub to drink in. We got settled in there but it wasn't long before the Old Bill found us and wouldn't let us leave the pub. The whole day was a complete waste of time.

I've also received a few Banning Orders from the courts plus I've had

3 Life Bans from football, from the club and the police. The last one was for the row with Hibs when I was banned from every football ground in Scotland. The other one was for P.S.V. Eindhoven in Holland for which I got another Life Ban and there was a third Life Ban. Officially I'm not allowed into Ibrox but if I'm with the kids the police will no do anything. They'd sort of turn a blind eye. The police obviously don't like certain people but I get on all right with them. The way I look at it is they're just doing their job. The ones in the job now are fair but the old lot were a different breed. For instance, take the trouble with P.S.V. One of them in his report said he saw 18 of us lot fighting and could name us. He must have had some eyesight to see and name 18 people fighting all at the same time. Don't forget there were hundreds of people involved and it was dark? When this bloke moved on the new lot that replaced him even said he'd been well out of order and said they'd never do anything like that, and so far they've been true to their word.

How I ended finding Peterborough and living down there was strange, it all started when I went down there to meet me good mates, Brooney and Smoothie. Twenty five of us were going down to watch Chelsea at home to Middlesbrough and they then moved the game from a Saturday to a Sunday so we had a look at that Saturday's fixtures and saw Peterborough were at home to Bristol City, so we decided to still go down to London and stop off on the way and have a look around in Peterborough. We got in a pub and got chatting to some of the locals who told us both Bristol clubs, City and Rovers had been going there for years and took the piss.

Next thing there's a mob of Bristol City outside the pub. We're straight out and straight into them. They've bolted and we've chased them down the road. At the bottom of the road was a line of Old Bill and the Bristol mob has got the other side of the coppers and told them we'd just chased them. "Fuck the Old Bill" we said, and went straight through the Old Bill and carried on chasing this Bristol firm. They were shitting themselves.

That night it was on a few of the hooligan websites on the Internet asking who the mad Jocks were that were with Peterboro. These cunts on the internet make me laugh. They're Internet warriors. They can't fight at football so they fight with words and they spill and spew out their bollocks on their computers. They must live at home with their mums and sit in their bedrooms with their Stone Island jumpers on giving it the large until Mummy calls them for their tea and watch the Chuckle Brothers or Tracey Beaker, with their tea on a tray in front of the telly. Sad cunts that's all they are, the sort of people that believe everything Dougie Brimson says. Just because you wear the clobber it doesn't make you a face.

A lot of people up here associate with the wearing of something Stone Island with being a football hooligan but it's just trendy and fashionable. A lot of ordinary Joe Bloggs types wear it though because it's smart. Looking smart at football is all part of the thing. Football, fashion and music all go together. Don't let anyone tell you different. It's not just about the fighting and the violence.

Me now personally I seldom go to the football. I keep in touch with everyone and speak to a few of the boys on the phone but it doesn't bother me now. I'm keeping my head down and working hard. I like my holiday's abroad and I've been away with my mate, Warren, and his family to Grand Canaria. I'm still into the music and one of my mates up in Edinburgh has bought an old cinema and turned it into a music venue. It's the bollocks, a right good venue. I've recently been to see `Snow Patrol` and I saw Eminem at Hampden. I also saw Hard-fi up here and they were good. They're Brentford supporters who come from over West London way. Yes, I'm still into the music scene but now I'm chilled out and I ain't misbehaving.

CHAPTER 11

THE SONGS

THE SASH MY FATHER WORE

Sure I'm an Ulster Orangeman, from Erin's Isle I came
To see my British brethren, all of honour and of fame
And to tell them of my forefathers who fought in days of yore
That I might have the right to wear the sash my father wore.

CHORUS

It is old but it is beautiful and its colours they are fine
It was worn at Derry, Aughrim, Enniskillen and the Boyne
My father wore it as a youth in bygone days of yore
And on the Twelfth I love to wear the sash my father wore

For those brave men who crossed the Boyne have not fought or died
   in vain
Our Unity, Religion, Laws and Freedom to maintain,

If the call should come we'll follow the drum and cross that river
    once more
That tomorrow's Ulster man may wear the sash my father wore.

And when some day across the sea to Antrim's shore you come
We'll welcome you in royal style to the sound of flute and drum
And Ulster's hills shall echo still from Rathlin to Dromore
As we sing again the loyal strain of The Sash My Father Wore.

Y.C.V. (YOUNG CITIZEN VOLUNTEERS)

Oh! Father why are you so sad this first of July morn
When Ulster men are proudly glad of the land where they were
    born?
Oh! Son I see in memory of the things that used to be
When being just a lad like you, I joined the Y.C.V.

From the hill and glens the call to arms was heard by one and all
And from the glens came brave young men to answer Ulster's call
'Twas long ago we faced the foe, the Y.C.V. and me
And by my side they fought and died that Ulster might be free.

So now my son I've told you why on July morn I sigh
For I recall my comrades all on darkest days gone by
I recall the men who fought in the glen with rifle and grenade
May heaven keep the men that sleep in the Y.C.V. Brigade.

A FATHER'S ADVICE

Said a father to his son
"Oh my boy the time has come, our country is calling unto thee
For those rebels once again, to unite us is their aim
And together we must stand to keep her free."

CHORUS

Remember our fathers brave and bold
As they fought for Ulster's cause in far off lands
My father said to me I must join the Y.C.V.
With a rifle or a pistol in my hand.

From Belfast to Armagh
Loughall to old Crossgar
From Ballymena to old Omagh Town
With their standards flying high
As it was in days gone by
We will rally round the flag for liberty.

CHORUS

BLUE SEA OF IBROX

I've sailed the wide Atlantic
Crossed the deep Pacific shores
I've sailed around the stormy capes
And heard the Forties roar
I've plied the Indian Ocean
Crossed the deep blue China Sea

But there's a sea back home in Scotland
That means more than all the rest to me.

CHORUS

It's the blue, blue blue sea of Ibrox
It's the greatest sight that I have ever seen
It's the blue, blue, blue sea of Ibrox
And it happens when the Orange beats the Green

No more I'll said the seven seas
No more I'll ever roam
No more I'll feel the urge again
I'm back where I belong

At 3 o'clock each Saturday
I'll join the mighty throng
With flags and banners all around
You'll hear me sing this song.

CHORUS

HANDS ACROSS THE WATER

Just across the Irish Sea
Stirs a heart of loyalty
Raised in honour and in dignity
Drives a will to keep us British free
Not alone are we on this journey
For in a land just across the sea
Is a hand that reaches out in friendship
And a bond that's lasted centuries.

And its hands across the water
Reaching out for you and me
For Queen, for Ulster and for Scotland
Helps to keep our loyal people free
Let the cry be "No Surrender"
Let no-one doubt this loyalty
Reaching out to the brave Red Hand of Ulster
Is the hand across the sea.

CHICKEN SUPPER

Could you go a chicken supper Bobby Sands?
Could you go a chicken supper Bobby Sands?
Could you go a chicken supper
You dirty Fenian fucker
Could you go a chicken supper Bobby Sands?

Could you go a can of Coke to wash it down?
Could you go a can of Coke to wash it down?
Could you go a can of Coke?
I hope you fucking choke
Could you go a can of Coke to wash it down?

HERE LIES A SOLDIER

In dungeon deep I know what fate awaits me
Tied hand and foot, the foe has bound me fast
And in my pain I pray my God above me
Will grant this wish I know will be my last.

Don't bury me in Erin's Fenian valley
Take me home to Ulster, let me rest
And on my gravestone carve this simple message
Here lies a soldier of the U.V.F.

CHORUS

Here lies a soldier, here lies a soldier
Who fought and died for what he thought was best
Here lies a soldier, here lies a soldier,
Here lies a soldier of the U.V.F.

So gently drape the Red Hand round my shoulders
Pin no heroes' medals on my chest
But if they ask you, will you kindly tell them
Here lies a soldier of the U.V.F.

CHORUS

Whenever I'm in times of trouble
Mother Mary comes to me
Singing Glasgow Celtic 1, Caley 3
Celtic 1, Caley 3
Celtic 1, Caley 3
Singing Glasgow Celtic 1, Caley 3

We are Rangers, we are Rangers
No-one likes us, we don't care
We hate Celtic, Fenian bastards
And we'll chase them anywhere

Hullo, hullo,
We are the Billy boys

Hullo, Hullo,
You'll know us by our noise
We're up to our necks in Fenian blood
Surrender or you'll die
For we are the Bridgeton Derry boys

No Pope and no Rome
No Chapels to sadden my eyes
No Nuns and No Priests
Fuck you Rosary beads
Every day is the 12th of July

SCRAPBOOK

EXCLUSIVE

CASUAL BATTLE BUSES SHOCK!

By IAIN FERGUSON

A FLEET of buses have been booked by Hibs casuals for Sunday . . . their destination unknown.

But today the Record can reveal the coaches, carrying as many as 300 mem-bers of the Capital City Service, are heading for the Scottish League Cup Final with Rangers at Parkhead.

And they hope to have a showdown with the notorious Inter City Firm.

Yesterday, Andy Blance, one of the leaders of the Hibs casuals, told of his battle plans for Sunday.

Both Strathclyde and Lothians police are aware of the casuals' plans and are mounting one of the biggest ever operations in a bid to prevent the violence.

And they will attempt to STOP the busloads of Hibs casuals BEFORE they reach their destination.

An insider told the Record: "We know buses have been booked by Hibs casuals, stating false destinations. We will be doing everything we can to

Turn to Page Five

BLANCE . . . Out of jail only three weeks ago but going to the game

London thugs get the blame

RANGERS fans claimed they had been infiltrated by thugs from London.

Tommy Sinclair, 47, of Govan, said: "When people came running out of Digby's bar some of the lads in Rangers colours had Cockney accents.

"Some were chanting 'ICF, ICF'.

Trouble

"They were obviously from the Inter City Firm, the thugs that follow some London clubs.

"The people who did this were not proper fans.

"The sooner they are kicked out of the club the better.

"There were definitely English fans among the ones who went out looking for trouble."

A police spokesman said: "We know people travelled from all over the country to watch Rangers."

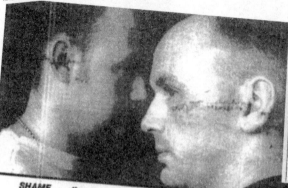

SHAME . . . the scars of the two brothers slashed in Sunderland

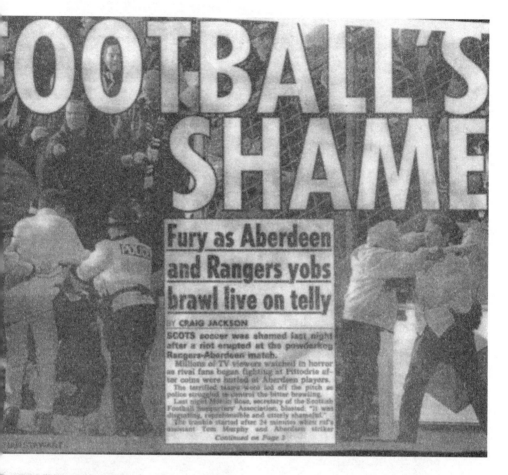

FOOTBALL'S SHAME

Fury as Aberdeen and Rangers yobs brawl live on telly

BY CRAIG JACKSON

SCOTS soccer was shamed last night after a riot erupted at the powderkeg Rangers-Aberdeen match.

Millions of TV viewers watched in horror as rival fans began fighting at Pittodrie after coins were hurled at Aberdeen players.

The terrified teams were led off the pitch as police struggled to control the bitter brawling.

Last night Malish Ross, secretary of the Scottish Football Supporters' Association, blasted: "It was disgusting, reprehensible and utterly shameful."

The trouble started after 24 minutes when ref's assistant Tom Murphy and Aberdeen striker

Continued on Page 3

MINDLESS MORONS

Continued from Page 1

Robbie Winters complained they were being pelted with coins at an Aberdeen corner.

Ref Mike McCurry stopped the game and asked security staff to lay on extra protection.

But as Winters went to take the corner again, Sky cameras clearly showed him being hit on the back of the head with a 50p piece thrown from a crowd of Rangers yobs.

As police and Rangers ace Lorenzo Amoruso pleaded for calm, 20 Aberdeen louts charged the Rangers hooligans, and one Gers fan was left bleeding after being hit on the back of the head.

As blood poured from his wound, two terrified female Gers supporters were led away by McCurry then ushered both teams off for their own safety.

Rangers' Operations Executive Laurence MacIntyre begged fans to calm down so the game could

...nters clutches head after coin attack

HUMAN SHIELD: Riot cops surround pitch perimeter before game restarts

go on while heavily protected riot squad police ringed the stand holding the Gers thugs — who then started "fighting among THEMSELVES.

The game eventually restarted 17 minutes later as police restored order to the 20,000 crowd.

The riot is the worst violence at a Scots game since Hugh Dallas was felled by a coin at the Old Firm match at Parkhead in 1999.

Last night Scottish Premier League supremo Roger Mitchell blasted: "Despite the strenuous efforts of police, security staff and club officials, a mindless minority of morons engaged in behaviour which will sicken any true football fan.

"We utterly condemn the behaviour of the small minority in both sets of fans."

He said the SPL would launch a probe and warned: "Future matches between Aberdeen and Rangers may kick off in the early afternoon."

Sports pundit Charlie Nicholas raged: "What chance have we got of getting Euro 2008? Forget it, if this is the way things are going to materialise."

Fans' chief Martin Rose added: "These shameful scenes have to be bitterly condemned.

"People should be going to watch the game, not to to indulge in that kind of disgusting and reprehensible behaviour."

He added: "We all hoped we'd turned a corner when it came to football violence. This proves the menace is back."

Cops also had to break up fighting between rival fans in Aberdeen's Marketgate before the game.

In total, there was one arrest inside the ground and 13 before the game. Nine people received minor injuries during the fracas.

HATE: See Score and Back Page

Police call for stadium ban on soccer casuals

By Alex Robertson
Crime Reporter

CONVICTED football casuals must be banned from grounds across Scotland to curb a rise in hooliganism, it was claimed today.

Senior officers in Strathclyde Police believe the time has come to introduce banning orders and are expected to call on the Scottish Executive to introduce new laws.

The call comes after eight casuals pled guilty at Glasgow Sheriff Court following a running battle between Rangers and Aberdeen fans in the city centre.

Scotland's largest force says banning orders will tackle the hardcore who are using football rivalry as an excuse for violence.

Around 50 hooligans are awaiting trial following a number of clashes across Scotland.

In the west of Scotland, gangs of between 30 and 50 people are attaching themselves to clubs.

The gangs include Rangers Inter City Firm.

SECURITY CHIEF: the SFA's Willie McDougall

Celtic Soccer Crew, Motherwell Saturday Service, St Mirren Love Street Division and Airdrie Section B.

They are mostly made up of young men who have joined forces with hardened casuals.

Banning orders are in place in England and Wales and prevent convicted hooligans travelling to sporting grounds across Europe.

Around 2500 England fans will be prevented from travelling to Portugal for Euro 2004.

Superintendent Kenneth Scott works in G division which covers Ibrox Stadium and Hampden.

He said that while individual clubs can take action, the police need the power to ban people on a wider scale.

"We start from the same position in every game and can't prevent known hooligans entering a football ground."

Around 100 football casuals are understood to join forces and follow the national side and have caused trouble at Euro 96 in England and the World Cup in France in 1998.

Willie McDougall, SFA security chief and former Strathclyde Police chief, said: "In Scotland, intelligence-gathering is good and there is a minority of supporters who are bad guys.

"The SFA welcomes anything that helps eradicate football disorder."

Last year, the European Union recommended all member states ban people who are guilty of violent conduct at sporting events.

A Scottish Executive spokeswoman said it would consider what action "might be required" once details on the situation were submitted by the Association of Chief Police Officers.

The police would be responsible for administering banning orders.

alex.robertson@
eveningtimes.co.uk

SCARED MUM HELPS IN THUG CRACKDOWN

By IAN METCALFE

SCOTS football casual's mum elping police sh the thugs' ork.

e Edinburgh n fears her son d be killed or ed if their reign ror isn't ended.

she has passed on ation about their es to a London-olice team work-ing to stamp them out.

The woman says her son – now in his early 20s – became hooked on hooliganism when he was just 16.

And she claims the football casuals are also into:

● DRUG dealing – even smuggling them into a Scottish prison.

● LAUNDERING forged £20 notes, making big profits.

● AND getting involved on the fringes of fascist groups and the IRA.

"The whole casuals movement is a lot bigger than people – including the police – think it is," she said.

"And I want to see it stopped before someone else's son – maybe mine – dies."

She slammed police and clubs for not doing enough, saying the authorities "turned a blind eye" because most of the trouble was away from the grounds.

The woman said Hibs casuals were Irish republican supporters.

"I don't know of their exact IRA links but I've been told that if they wanted guns they could get them," she added.

scort Rangers fans to Aberdeen Station after the match

LE flared following the n v Rangers match on y as more than 100 ns gathered at the

quickly called for and about 40 officers rted by the dog unit – d to control and dis-e crowd quickly. al arrests were made and officers said inquiries were continuing to identify those involved in the disturbance.

Officers said the so-called "casual" supporters of both clubs were involved.

They said the trouble-makers, who were not dressed in football regalia, were involved in a few scuffles and began throwing coins and other mis-siles, although no one was injured. A spokesman said: "Some casuals had gone down to the beach area and there was a confrontation but it was pretty short-lived.

"The area was heavily po-liced, so there was not much of a chance for anything to hap-pen."

One female witness, who was at the beach with a friend, said: "We had just gone to get an ice-cream and something had obviously happened as a load of people came running out of Cafe Continental and started clashing with police. Then more officers came along with big, scary dogs and the police got it under control quickly."

Supporters of both clubs were out in force for the Pitod-drie game, which kicked off the new season. Aberdeen lost 3-0.

Police said a dozen people were arrested for minor of-fences including drunkenness. Some of them are expected to appear at Aberdeen Sheriff Court today.

WHODUNNIT?

Rangers fall out with cops over thug fans

A WAR of words erupted last night between officials o Rangers and English police chiefs after the Ibro> club blamed a LONDON gang – and not Scots fans – foi last week's scenes of violence in Sunderland.

But a top policeman in the north east of England town said he hadNC EVIDENCE of organised infiltration by casual gangs.

And he said SIXTEEN Scots were among the 47 arrests last Wednesday in Sunderland.

But last night Rangers security chief Alistair Hood claimed the club's fans were NOT TO BLAME for the savage violence.

Hood, a former police chief, was contacted by Rangers and Sunderland fans on Friday and travelled to Wearside on Sunday to interview English supporters. He said:

"There is now no doubt whatsoever that the street disturbances and serious assaults were orchestrated and committed by an organisation known as the Inter City Firm.

"It attaches itself to clubs in England, such as Chelsea and West Ham, and has no connection at all with Rangers Football Club.

WRONG

"I felt that I owed it to our fans to clarify the situation and refute the unwarranted and savage attack by the media and other authorities.

"Reports were inaccurate and distorted and, although I strongly deprecate the excessive drinking by fans of both clubs, before and after the match, I cannot stand by and allow the true Rangers fans to be pilloried for acts they did not commit.

"This illegal organisation, which has tenuous links within Scotland, is not football minded in any way."

And Mr Hood went on: "It is very hard for anyone not to retaliate when bottles, glasses and knives are being thrown at them.

"What I am saying is that this goes beyond football hooliganism which is a club reponsibility.

"This is organised crime."

But Superintendent

● Callers to the Record claim Rangers casuals meet in a city centre pub and target Celtic, Hibs and Aberdeen games.
On May Day, dressed in England tops, they hired a bus to go south and support Chelsea casuals, who have notorious fascist links.

By IAIN FERGUSON

Dennis Green, the commander of police for the Gary Bennet Testimonial at Roker Park, hit back, saying:

"Sixteen Scots were arrested for various public order offences out of a total of 47 arrests.

"There was a carnival atmosphere inside the ground but the majority of incidents took place before the match.

"If accusations of organised gangs infiltrating the fans and causing trouble are being made we would like to hear from people with evidence of that and from Rangers Football Club.

EASY

"We checked all buses and trains arriving in Sunderland and are satisfied they were all bona fide supporters organisations.

"There was certainly no evidence of ICF attendance at the match".

Brothers Gary and Stephen Marr were savagely slashed by thugs wearing Rangers shirts.

But last night 24-year-old Gary, who had to have 40 stitches to the Stanley knife wound across his cheek, said he could not tell where his attackers came from.

He said: "The lads who got me didn't stop to say anything – they just cut me.

"The pub was full of Rangers fans – they all wore their blue shirts and scarves.

"But anyone from Chelsea or West Ham could have easily mixed in."

SCOTS THUGS SHAME

More trouble erupted in the city centre with rival gangs congregating in Royal Exchange Square and George Square.

The Chief Constable also revealed that some English fans missed trains and British Rail were forced to put on extra transport.

Overall there were 260 arrests made – 100 English and 160 Scots.

Around 200 people were treated in hospitals throughout the city for injuries related to the football violence, but Mr Sloan said the amount was not abnormal.

He said that a considerable number of English fans had travelled to Glasgow with the intention of causing disorder and violence.

He compared the total number of arrests at the Rous Cup game with the 243 arrests over a full 24 hour period at the Rangers v Celtic Cup Final the previous week.

He said: "The arrests at the Scotland-England game were concentrated in a couple of hours before and after the match.

Mr Sloan added: "It was a difficult time for the community and for the police.

The Chief Constable declined to back the calls for the Scotland-England game to be banned and said that this was a matter for the football authorities.

He said his personal view was that the growth of family areas at football matches would be a major factor in containing hooliganism.

POLICE STUDYING THUGS ON VIDEO

HUNDREDS of hours of video footage of English and Scottish football hooligans will be examined by police today.

Detectives with the British Transport Police secretly filmed the fans as they gathered at Glasgow's Queen Street and Central stations on Saturday.

It is thought between 200 and 300 English casuals travelled by train. Now the tapes will be carefully scrutinised as part of a vital intelligence gathering operation.

Investigations will be made where video tape shows acts of violence or hooliganism by fans.

Officers will also try to identify known football hooligans caught in crowd scenes, and the information added to growing computer files on Britain's violent fans.

More than 200 fans – half of them English – are being held in police cells. Glasgow Sheriff Court is preparing to deal with the huge numbers expected to appear tomorrow.

Barmaid faces fury of the mob

DRUNKEN Rangers fans terrorised a pub manageress as they struggled to get more drink.

They warned Michelle Muir: "Keep serving or else."

She said: "They were ten-deep at the bar and I decided to try and close up because of the rowdiness.

"Fighting broke out between Rangers fans in the bar.

"Most were frustrated when they couldn't get drink because we were so busy.

"I was told there would be trouble if I stopped serving."

STOLEN

The pub – next door to Sunderland's Roker Park ground – also had £50 stolen from the till.

By BRIAN McCARTNEY

Michelle added: "I had to wait for an hour before the police arrived and by then they were almost uncontrollable."

Trouble started five hours before kick-off to the supposed friendly.

Fans high on drink stole cars, smashed windows, battled in the streets and robbed shops.

Innocent passers-by were also assaulted as the drunken yobboes brought shame on Rangers and Scotland.

would either after seeing the mayhem.

"There were several appalling incidents of disorder and violence.

"I have written a full report on the disturbances and it will be sent to the FA."

The game was arranged as a benefit match for Sunderland star Gary Bennett.

He said: "It is very sad that there was trouble on what was otherwise a tremendous night."

Police match commander Supt Dennis Green said: "If that's how the Scottish fans behave during a friendly I wouldn't like to see them when they mean business.

"I would not welcome them back for a friendly or any other kind of fixture and I doubt any match commander in England

SHAME

The English disease travels nort
on Scottish football day of disgrac

By **Iain Macfarlane**

during the game

THE new wave of football violence that has disgraced English football spread to Scotland last night when fans clashed during Aberdeen's match with Rangers at Pittodrie.

Shameful clashes between rival fans, which erupted midway through the first half, were beamed across the world, dragging Scottish football into the gutter.

The tinderbox SPL match was held up for 17 minutes after missiles were thrown from the Rangers fans towards Aberdeen player Robbie Winters.

He was hit on the back of the head by a coin as he was about to take a corner kick. There had already been a number of missiles thrown on to the pitch.

Rangers star Lorenzo Amoruso immediately tried to calm the visit-

ing supporters and refere McCurry reported the inc the police. He then orde players to leave the field tried to weed out the thug

Before Grampian Poli get into the crowd around gans from the Aberdeen through police lines and towards Rangers' fans.

Horrific scenes deve fights broke out and pol gled to regain control.

When the players had the field for eight minu gency police cover was into the ground in the officers in riot gear.

They formed a yellow the Pittodrie trackside a

TURN TO PAGE 6, C3(

Fan on CS gas charg

THIRTEEN fans - ten of them English - appeared on petition in private before Sheriff Graham Johnstone on charges considered more serious by the procurator fiscal.

Nineteen-year-old Jonathon David Sampson of The Travellers, Lavelock Road, Stanley, Wakefield, is alleged to have possessed "a weapon adapted for the discharge of noxious CS gas", contrary to the Firearms Act on Saturday in Pollokshaws Road near Eglinton Toll, possessed a firearm, namely a CS gas cannister, and committed a breach of the peace by discharging the CS cannister into a crowd.

David Carrick (24), of Croftbank Street, Springburn, Glasgow is alleged to have assault-

ed Graham Boner on Sunday in Hope Street near Argyle Street and struck him on the head and face with a chain or similar instrument to his severe injury.

Ian Johnston (32), no fixed abode, is alleged to have conducted himself in a disorderly manner and forming part of a group causing alarm and annoyance.

Mark Grierson (21), of Moonhill Drive South, Carlisle, Mark Boardman (19), of Mayhurst Avenue, Woking, Andrew McGovern (24), of Hewson Road, Lincoln and David Smith (22), of Bridges Avenue, Barry, Manchester face similar charges.

Steven Connellan (29), of Windsor Terrace,

Newbold, Rochdale, is alleged te ted a breach of the peace in Re Square on Saturday.

Sean Gibbs (17), of Heatherle Cheltenham, is alleged to have breach of the peace at Saracen Gallowgate, by obstructing the pav ing, swearing, singing and chantin

Adrian Porter (25), of Parlin Burnley, and Andrew Porter (22 Road, Luton, were charged with b peace and resisting arrest.

Two Scots, Scott Forbes (23) Terrace, Edinburgh, and James Mc Street, Leith, face breach of the pea

FACES OF HATE: Hendry, Chugg and Carrick try to look menacing as they are pictured being run out of Bordeaux after a sting operation involving Scots, Spanish and French police foiled their plot to cause violence at Scotland's game there this week

MARK HENDRY

NDRY is a 24-year-old who lives alone in a ncil flat in Shettleston, Glasgow, and is known ntelligence sources as a leading member of the er City Firm of football casuals. He travels to es all over Britain, meeting fellow ICF mem- s in a Glasgow city centre wine bar.

Hendry is a member of the British National ty and, with close friend Sandy Chugg, nomi- ed Robert Currie as the party's candidate for sgow Shettleston at the 1997 General Election.

He has two convictions – one for possession of gs in 1995 and one for a breach of the peace.

He is well known in the east end of Glasgow for ing with the drugs fraternity. Among his other tacts is Brian "Harkie" Harkness, a founder of ICF and a prominent figure in the BNP.

a criminal source in Glasgow said: "Hendry s himself as a major player in both the drug ne and the casuals. He can be seen cruising the ttleston area most days with his cronies and ing with a criminal element."

SANDY CHUGG

CHUGG is the leader of the 58-strong group who were detained in Salou. He had a promising future at 16 as a footballer with Rangers.

But in 1990 he was jailed for three years at Glasgow Sheriff Court for dealing in LSD and temazepam.

He served two years of the sentence and although he has no criminal convictions since he is known to criminal intelligence officers as a main player in the Rangers casuals, the Inter City Firm.

Chugg, 26, enrolled at North Glasgow College in 1996 on an HND course in sports coaching which he is due to finish in the next few weeks.

Through the college, he was asked to supervise SFA coaching sessions in Cumbernauld for young footballers and was highly rated by coaches there.

He lives in a council flat in Shettleston, Glasgow but regularly visits his mother Margaret, 63, who lives in Duke Street in the east end of the city.

He has recently been spotted by police at matches in the north-east of England.

DAVID CARRICK

CARRICK, 32, is the "first lieutenant" of the ICF in the west of Scotland. Originally from the Springburn area of Glasgow, he moved three years ago to Kirkintilloch, near the city, where he lives in a council flat with a family called Findlay.

Carrick was cleared in 1989 of a brutal chain attack on an England football fan in Glasgow city centre. He later lost his job as an auxiliary nurse.

He now finances his many trips to England with the ICF from his wages as a panel beater.

He was present at one of the ICF's most infa- mous incidents in 1993 at Sunderland when two locals were slashed during running battles in the city before a Sunderland v Rangers testimonial match.

Carrick is close to some Edinburgh-based casu- als including shop owner James 'Fat' McLeod, 27, and his business partner David Keddie.

He also mixes with a Leith casual, Billy Archibald, who drives a BMW. McLeod, Keddie and Archibald were all with Carrick in Salou.

BOOT THEM OUT SAYS BOSS

RANGERS supremo David Murray vowed today: "We will boot out the troublemakers."

And he blamed a minority of "idiots" for damaging the reputation of the Ibrox club.

The Rangers chief executive said: "I am obviously very disappointed by the reports I have been hearing.

"If they are confirmed, we will be taking appropriate action.

"People who have been involved will not be back at Ibrox. We may have to reconsider our position about playing matches in England.

"I await a full report from the police. But rest assured, action will be taken against those involved.

"Regrettably, it seems some idiots have tarnished the club's reputation."

The Ibrox chief did not attend the friendly and is awaiting reports from club officials and police.

DAVID MURRAY: Vo

will take the severest a tion against them.

"Neither the player management nor myse learned of the scale of th problem until we hear reports this morning.

"Everyone at the clu is deeply distressed tha these people have let th side down.

"I am aware man Rangers fans were in En gland, either living ther or on holiday. But w will have to wait fo court appearances to e tablish where they com from."

ENGLISH THUGS 'BEHIND RIOTS'

RANGERS security chief Alister Hood yesterday blamed last week's Sunderland soccer riots on outlawed English thugs.

He travelled back to the town to quiz locals after he was flooded with calls from Rangers fans insisting: "We weren't to blame." Hood said: "There is now no doubt the street disturbances and serious assaults were orchestrated and committed by The Inter City Firm.

"This illegal organisation attaches itself to English clubs like Chelsea and West Ham and has no connection with

Shock

Rangers security boss Alistair Hood said the club was in a state of shock.

"We have gone seven years with almost no problems from our supporters and now this has happened in one night.

"We don't know exactly how many Rangers suporters are among those arrested but when we find who they are we

---

How dare English hooligans wear our strips . . .

RANGERS top fan last night slammed Chelsea hooligans for wearing Ibrox jerseys.

Brawlers were seen clearly on TV in Rangers outfits as hundreds of Chelsea yobs rioted.

The mad scenes took place after Middlesbrough dumped the Londoners into the Second Division at Stamford Bridge on Saturday.

Hooligans

Police and Middlesbrough fans were lashed with bottles and stones and there were 34 arrests in the ground. It took 30 minutes to restore order and the 7000 visiting fans were locked in the ground for almost an hour for their own safety.

Rangers manager Graeme Souness was at the game watching Middlesbrough's centre back Gary Pallister, before flying to Majorca for a sunshine break with his family.

IT IS VIRTUALLY CERTAIN THAT THE CHELSEA THUGS HAVE BLOCKED ENGLAND'S RE-ENTRY TO EUROPE NEXT SEASON.

Rangers officials were not available yesterday but David Miller, from Kilsyth, secretary of the powerful Rangers Supporters Association said:

"Rangers fans do not want to be associated with hooligans.

"*I don't believe it was Rangers fans who were involved at Stamford Bridge. If they were they will be answerable to us.*

"Our branches are all closed for the summer so there could be no organised trip to London.

"Our kit can be bought in shops all over the country. Chelsea fans have been to see Rangers in the past and have been to our social club without causing trouble."

The Ibrox club must now

ALEX CAMERON reporting

worry about the chance of English fans in Rangers shirts causing trouble during the European Championships in West Germany next month.

SFA President David Will, who sits on UEFA's executive said yesterday: "I would hate to think any Scottish club will be brought into this by English fans wearing their strips.

Chances

"*THE SCENES IN LONDON WILL HAVE BEEN SEEN ON TV ALL OVER EUROPE. CLEARLY, THIS IS VERY HARMFUL.*"

"However, the behaviour of English fans during the European

Championships month could be the ing factor."

English FA boss Millichip admitted: another nail. And o occasion it may be this one i exaggerated."

Other clubs outraged by this l thuggery .

Martin Edwards, man of Manchester U who hope to be in E next season fired: appalling this 1 disgraceful perform at Chelsea should the chances of those who have been pe well behaved."

"Unfortunately w don't know how damage they have and can only keep fi crossed and hop noted there has be trouble at Old Traff

PLAY-OFF SCO
SHINE – Page 3

NO HIDING PLACE . . . a Rangers top is clearly visible at Chelsea on Saturday.

WE'LL CRUSH THE CASUALS

POLICE READY FOR ENGLISH THUGS

By ARNOT McWHINNIE

THE cop in charge of one of Scotland's biggest anti-hooligan operations vowed yesterday: "We'll crush the English casuals."

Strathclyde's Assistant Chief Constable John Dickson is the man who has been given the task of making Hampden a trouble-free zone today.

And most of the region's 7000-strong police force will be involved.

The police were caught on the hop two years ago by thugs from the south out to cause mayhem.

But they warned yesterday: "It won't happen again."

At a Press conference Mr Dickson revealed that after the battles at the last Scotland-England international, his force set-up an extensive intelligence network with forces throughout Britain.

Now the movements of English soccer gangs are being plotted and monitored.

Mr Dickson said: "They may have more surprises for us, but we have one or two surprises for them also."

He refused, however, to reveal details of the sting in the tail.

But he promised thugs they would be dealt with "quickly and effectively".

Some of the tactics which the police will employ are:

POLICE "spotters" from all over Britain monitoring trouble-makers.

ENGLISH supporters buses being met as they cross the border and guided off the motorway near Glasgow straight to Hampden.

UNDERCOVER officers travelling on trains.

Mr Dickson warned thugs that two years ago Scottish courts cracked down with jail sentences of up to four years.

But he also took time to welcome decent English supporters and appealed to all fans to help police by pointing out rowdies,

RIFKIND SCORNS BAN ON MATCH

SCOTS Secretary Malcolm Rifkind yesterday dismissed calls to ban the Scotland – England football international.

And he also scorned suggestions that an English style ID card scheme should be introduced in Scotland.

By DAVE KING

But at the same time Scots Sports Minister Michael Forsyth was calling for a report on the Hampden battle.

Mr Rifkind said that the fan behaviour in Scotland was of a very high standard, despite the incidents.

INSTANT

He added: "As far as the question of a ban is concerned, that is just premature hype."

And he attacked Cathcart MP John Maxton who had called for a ban on the game.

The Scots Secretary said: "I do not believe that instant demands are a sensible response to the problem."

And he went on: "We have ruled out ID cards for the foreseeable future."

But yesterday Michael Forsyth, who attended the match, said: "I am asking for a full report from the police and seeking advice about the future of the match."

LAST NIGHT regional councillor for King's Park and Aikenhead Bill Millar slammed Scots fans as well as English – AND the national stadium.

He said: "The fans with the kilt and the Scottish strip intimidate the English. They are every bit as bad.

"And how can you expect good behaviour when Hampden is the way it is?

"If you have a park like a pigsty, then pigs will cause trouble."

TODAY more than 200 fans, half of them English, will appear in Glasgow courts in connection with Saturday's incidents.

INTER CITY FIRM (HOOLIGAN MONTHLY No.1)

WELCOME BACK TO ALL OUR MEMBERS BOTH FROM LAST SEASON AND TO ALL THE LADS
WHO HAVE DECIDED TO MAKE A COMEBACK THERE IS A LOT OF YOU WE HAVEN'T SEEN
IN A FEW SEASONS.
THOSE OF YOU WHO ATTENDED THE MAN.UNITED GAME WILL AGREE THAT ALTHOUGH WE
HAD ENOUGH LADS TO DO THEM OUR ORGANIZATION WASN'T UP TO SCRATCH
NOW IN THIS SEASON 90 THINGS ARE ABOUT CHANGE ....
 OUR FIRST GAME IS A SNIDEY ONE AGAINST DUNFERMLINE THEN FOLLOWS ON TWO
AWAY VISITS TO EDINBURGH THE FIRST AGAINST ARGUABLY NO.1 WITH OURSELVES
HIBS WHO ON A RECENT VISIT TO LONDON CLAIMED THEY DID MILLWALL AND EVEN
GOT SOME PUBLICITY THEN ITS HEARTS (THE MOB ALLERGIC TO GLASGOW) AND IM
SURE THEYRE STILL WONDERING WHAT HIT THEM ON OUR LAST VISIT TO THE GORGIE
ON OUR TRIP TO THE HIBS GAME THERE WILL BE TWO BUSES BEING RUN, THOSE OF
YOU WHO GO FOR A BOX WILL KNOW WHERE AND WHEN SO LETS GET A DECENT MOB.

ON THE HEARTS GAME WE WILL DISCUSS THE ARRANGEMENTS FOR THE BIG GAME
AGAINST THE SCUM (LETS HOPE THEY BRING A BIGGER MOB THAN THEIR LAST
TRIP) SO LETS HAVE A GOOD TURN OUT AND FINISH THESE BEGGARS OFF ONCE AND
FOR ALL...
AND A BIT OF GOOD NEWS AFTER WE DISPOSE OF KILLIE IN THE CUP WE FACE THE
HIBEES AT IBROX ON 4th OF SEPTEMBER SO LETS SEE HOW GOOD THE HIBS REALLY
ARE.....

NOW FOR A BIT OF SLAGGING:-

UTILITY   - ONE OF THE BIGGEST MOBS OUT BUT WHEN IT COMES TO BOXING WHAT
A JOKE

M.S.S.   - SAID THEY WERE MAKING A COMEBACK BUT WE ARE STILL WAITING

L.S.D.   - THE BIGGEST CRAPBAGS IN THE WHOLE OF SCOTLAND

A.F.C.   - TOO BUSY SHEEP SHAGGING AND WRITING BOOKS FOR ANYTHING ELSE

C.S.C   - THE FILTHIEST BUNCH OF BEGGARS IN THE U.K.

THE PARS - TOO SCARED OF US GLASGA BOYS AND STILL CRYING ABOUT BIG JIM

C.C.S   - THREATENING WALLACE WITH THEIR VODA-PHONE AND STARTING
RUMOURS ABOUT HOW GOOD THEY ARE TO THE SUN.

C.C.F   - USE TO HAVE A MOB WHICH COULD TRAVEL BUT AFTER THE TANKING
THEY GOT AT ST.ENOCH SQUARE THEY HAVE NEVER BEEN THE SAME

CONGRATULATIONS TO ST.JOHNSTONE FOR MAKING IT UP WITH THE BIG BOYS AND
ALTHOUGH WE SMASHED THEM IN THE CUP LAST SEASON WE'RE SURE THEY WILL
STILL MANAGE TO TRAVEL TO IBROX AND AS FOR DUNDEE WHAT DIFFERENCE DOES IT
MAKE THE UTILITY WAS DUNDEE AND DUNDEE UTD MIXED IN TOGETHER.
LETS HOPE CHELSEA CAN MAKE IT UP TO MORE GAMES AND PROVE THE ENGLISH
CONNECTION TO BE VERY SUCCESSFUL.
THIS LEAFLET WAS MADE IN THE EAST END AND WILL BE PRINTED EVERY MONTH SO
AFTER YOU READ THIS GET IT COPIED AND PASS ONE ON.

INTER CITY FIRM (HOOLIGAN MONTHLY NO.2)

WELCOME TO ISSUE NUMBER 2 IN OUR HIGHLY SUCCESSFUL MONTHLY LEAFLET, WE WILL
START BY SAYING CONGRATULATIONS TO ALL MEMBERS WHO HAVE BEEN WITH   US FOR
OUR FIRST MONTH IN THE LEAGUE. I'M SURE YOU WILL AGREE THAT SLOWLY BUT
SURELY THINGS ARE GETTING MORE ORGANIZED WEEK BY WEEK.

NOW DOWN TO BUSINESS ...WE'RE SURE YOU HAVE ALL READ ALL ABOUT HIBS THE
SUPPOSEDLY NO.1 OUTFIT IN SCOTLAND IN THE TIMES ALL ABOUT HOW 400 THUGS
WERE COLLECTING DOSH AND TRAVELLING ALL AROUND EUROPE....
 WELL WHERE WERE THEY IN THERE HOME TERRITORY WHEN 100 OF THE FIRM RAN
RIOTS THROUGH PRINCESS STREET DOOD THEM IN EASTER ROAD AND THEN GOT A LIFT
BACK TO OUR BUSES. THIS JUSTIFYS WHO REALLY IS NO.1 IN SCOTLAND AND THOSE
OF YOU WHO TURNED UP THAT DAY WILL PROBABLY NEVER FORGET IT (WHAT A DAY
OUT..HA..HA..HIBS).
AND ON THE SAME SUBJECT .. WE ARE SO FED UP TRAVELLING UP TO TYNECASTLE AND
NOT GETTING A BOX WHAT EVER HAPPENED TO HEARTS THEIR SO CALLED PITCH
INVASION(EASTER ROAD)WAS STARTED BY A DRUNK SCARFER THIS MOB CERTAINLY HAVE
GOT A BRASS NECK THEY OUGHT TO CALL IT A DAY AND PACK IT IN.

OUR FRIENDS ACROSS THE CITY ...YES THATS RIGHT THE SCUM
THAT MOB ARE STILL RUNNING ABOUT THE GORBALS LOOKING FOR THEIR BOTTLE (WELL
THE ONES THEY CAN THROW ANYWAY) WE HUMILIATED THIS MOB ON THE BRIDGE THEN
RATTLED THEM THROUGH THE FLATS(CATHOLIC LAND HA..HA..).
A MERE FIFTY OF THEM WERE BRAVE ENOUGH TO SHOW UP AT IBROX AND ITS A DAY
THEY WILL WANT TO FORGET.

OUR NEXT GAMES AHEAD IS AS FOLLOWS
DUNDEE UTD   (AWAY) 22ND SEPT
ABERDEEN   (HAMPDEN)25TH
MOTHERWELL   (HOME) 29TH
VALLETA   (HOME) 3RD OCT
ABERDEEN   (AWAY) 6TH
ST.MIRREN   (HOME) 13TH
ST.JOHNSTONE   (AWAY) 20TH

HEARTS' TOP BOY

AND THOSE OF YOU WHO MET STRANRAER IN CENTRAL WILL WANT TO SAY HELLO TO
THEM AGAIN THERE BACK UP IN COURT AGAIN IN NOV 17TH.
NOW ITS THIS TIME OF THE YEAR AGAIN RANGERS ARE IN EUROPE AND WE WILL WANT
TO SHOW THAT ALTHOUGH WE ARE NO.1 IN SCOTLAND WE WISH TO BE RECOGNIZED
THROUGH OUT EUROPE AS A FORCE TO BE RECKONED WITH.
AND EVEN ALTHOUGH THE LIVERPOOL GAME IS STILL A WHILE AWAY WE HAVE STARTED
GETTING THINGS ORGINAZED ALREADY.
SO LETS GET A GOOD START BY GETTING EVERYONE TO TURN UP AT THE SEMI-FINAL
AGAINST THE SHEEP-SHAGGERS.... WE HAVEN'T SEEN THEM IN GLASGOW FOR A FEW
SEASONS.
JUST BEFORE WE GO... HERES SOMETHING TO THINK ABOUT HOW COME EVER TIME THE
FIRM ARE UP AT HIBS WE ARE THE ONLY ONES TO GET JAIL.
IS IT BECAUSE THE SCREWS ARE SCARED OF THEM OR IS IT A FAMILY
CONNECTION........   WE WONDER !

            IF YOU WANT TO BE ONE JOIN THE FIRM

INTER CITY FIRM
(NEWSFLASH)

CALLING ALL MEMBERS

AS YOU ALL KNOW, THIS WEEK BRINGS TWO OF THE SEASONS MOST IMPORTANT
GAMES FOR US. FIRSTLY THERE IS THE SMALL MATTER OF THE SKOL CUP
FINAL AGAINST THE SCUMBAGS AT HAMPDEN (SUN28 oct). CELTIC HAVE
BEEN RABELING ON FOR WEEKS ABOUT THIS PARTICULAR GAME. SO LETS GO
OUT AND KICK THIS SHIT ALL OVER THE STREETS OF GLASGOW. LETS HOPE
CELTIC STAND THIS TIME AND DON'T SHIT IT AS USUAL. ALSO A FINAL
MENTION TO CELTIC, GARY MCGUIRE's DEATH WAS FUCK ALL TO DO WITH US
BUT 2's UP ANYWAY. (ANOTHER ONE BITES THE DUST...)

ONTO THE NEXT SUBJECT

RECENT MATCHES FOR EXAMPLE (ABERDEEN 6/10/90) HAVE PRODUCED VERY
POOR NUMBERS. LET US REMIND YOU ALL THAT HIBS ARE AT IBROX ON
THE SATURDAY AFTER THE CELTIC MATCH. BUT MORE ABOUT THAT LATER ON.
WE MUST STRESS THAT A VAST IMPROVEMENT MUST BE MADE OR WE WILL
FALL INTO THE SAME CATERGORY OF SO CALLED MOBS SUCH AS CELTIC,
HEARTS, etc. WE PROVED EARLIER IN THE SEASON AT EASTER RD. THAT
WE ARE STILL UNDISPUTED KINGS OF TERRACE VIOLENCE IN SCOTLAND.
THE PROUD NAME OF RANGERS INTER CITY FIRM IS FAST IN DANGER OF
BECOMING A JOKE. SO ALL FIRM MEMBERS GET YOUR FINGERS OUT YOUR
ARSES AND SORT IT OUT. THAT GOES TO ALL MOBS EAST END, SOUTH SIDE,
AND NORTH, EVERYWHERE.

NOW ONTO HIBS !

THE MEDIA DUBBED (CASUAL ARISTOCRATS) HIBS COME TO TOWN 3/11/90.
OUR MEMBERS IN THE EAST END HAVE RECEIVED INFORMATION FROM THE
EAST OF SCOTLAND THAT HIBS ARE PLANNING REVENGE FOR THE BRASS
NECK WE GAVE THEM AT EASTER RD. IN AUGUST. HIBS EXPECT TO CARRY
200 FOR THE MATCH. THEY ARE TARGETING PAISLEY ROAD WEST AS THE SITE
FOR THE KICK OFF. SO LETS GIVE HIBS GLASGOW's VERY BEST RECEPTION
AND PUT THE BASTARDS IN THERE PLACE. (2nd ASUSUAL) HA HA HA ....
PHONE EAST END BOYS FOR DETAILS. AND REMEMBER LARGE NUMBERS PLEASE.

FINALLY

BUSES FOR THE LIVERPOOL GAME ARE STILL ON, SO INFORMATION WILL BE
GIVEN. NAMES AND DEPOSITS TOOK AT HIBS MATCH. SIGNING OFF, LETS
HOPE TO BE TOASTING YET ANOTHER SKOL CUP SUCCESS ON AND OFF THE
FIELD WHEN HIBS HIT TOWN. SO KEEP THE FLAG FLYING.........

GLASGOW(CITY OF CULTURE).
1990.....

INTER CITY FIRM
A CLASS ABOVE THE REST

IN CONJUNCTION WITH
MAD SQUAD PRESS INC